Conceiving Evil

CONCEIVING EVIL

A Phenomenology of Perpetration

WENDY C. HAMBLET

Images by Martin Camarata

Algora Publishing
New York

Library of Congress Cataloging-in-Publication Data —

Hamblet, Wendy C., 1949-
    Conceiving evil: a phenomenology of perpetration / Wendy C. Hamblet.
        pages cm
    Includes bibliographical references and index.
        ISBN 978-1-62894-093-0 (soft cover: alk. paper) — ISBN 978-1-62894-094-
7 (hard cover: alk. paper) — ISBN 978-1-62894-095-4 (ebook) 1. Good and evil.
I. Title.
        BJ1401.H35 2014
        170—dc23
                                            2014025480

Printed in the United States

TABLE OF CONTENTS

PREFACE

Over the centuries, philosophers, theologians, religious cler-
ics—and in recent years even politicians and military profession-
als—investigate, talk, write, preach, and reproach others about
something they name "evil." People seem to agree that such a
thing as evil exists; they spend a great deal of energy discussing
the phenomenon of evil when they feel they have encountered
it, arguing for their favored meaning of the term and disputing
what does and does not constitute the real thing.

The term evil had all but fallen out of use in political and public discourse except in reference to the most egregious atrocities,
such as genocide. However, since the "September 11" attack on
the World Trade Center in New York, the language of evil has
again emerged, beginning with fundamentalist Christian United
States President George W. Bush, and later it echoed across the
globe in countries long thought too secular to fall into the serious use of such imagery.[1] Ironically, the new language was often
directed at those who had reintroduced it. The use of the archaic
and extreme imagery of evil by the leaders in enlightened democratic societies seems odd, archaic, medieval. But because in

---

1 Following the 9/11/2001 crisis, Canada's Minister of Defense, Richard
Hillier, took a hard and demonizing line, following George Bush's linguistic lead, and named enemy combatants in Afghanistan "evildoers"
and "scumbags." *Globe and Mail*, July 16, 2005.

democratic societies, leaders rise and fall according to public approval (admittedly, people are democratically powerful only one day every four years), framing their political and military agendas in the seductive language of evil can prove can prove highly efficacious, especially during times of national or social crisis. Modern leaders have begun to resort to the use of this extreme imagery because it can greatly enhance their appeal to popular audiences and serve effectively their political needs.

Why do the imagery and language of evil come to find place in modern secular societies? When crises befall people, they tend to lose their nuanced sense of reality and begin to see the world in more extreme terms—good guys and bad guys. Threat tends to makes people more conservative and more extreme in their view of the world. People in crisis begin frantically to try to make sense of their chaotic worlds, seeking ultimate and time-honored answers to explain the source of the crisis, because if one can locate the source, then the hope arises that the source can be eliminated.

The language and imagery of evil is so old, so potent, so persuasive, and so steeped in tradition that it can have a compelling effect upon troubled audiences. This explains why unscrupulous politicians and military spokespersons will rally the extreme language of evil during times of crisis to ignite people's fear and loathing of some enemy to serve their military and political designs. Whenever leaders use this archaic term, we may not know whether they are sincere (i.e., if their worldview truly includes a Manichean dichotomy of good and evil) or whether they are merely using the term for reasons of political expedience. However, when we see leaders using this imagery, we may be certain of two things. First, we may be confident that a declaration of war against some internal or external enemy is not far off, and second, we may be certain that it is time for a change of leadership.

In each of the varying differentiating centers of people's lives—spiritual, political, cultural, familial—where identities are constantly under construction, evil takes on a peculiar character that is meaningful within that existential space. The imagery of good and evil gives moral texture to life events and assigns the work of the god and the duties of the faithful disciple. Evil sometimes is understood as an abstract, absolute force inhabiting the universe or infecting it from a transcendent sphere of reality. Sometimes evil is distilled into a personified figure, a devil or demon, a political personage, or a foreign culture or civilization. Spinoza has his "Turks," Richard Hillier his "detestable scumbags" and "evildoers," and George W. Bush his "axis of evil". Sometimes evil is dissipated into a nebulous image or power within nature, a gnawing negative energy tainting an otherwise good world, a force associated with disease, untimely death, darkness, and chaos. The latter understanding undersits the philosophical dichotomy that has colored the history of ethical ideas—the idea that order and simplicity are good and disorder and complexity are bad—culminating in the belief that the enlightening force of knowledge is the secret to the expulsion of evil from the individual, from the decadent civilization, and from the human world. To paraphrase the Socratic dictum: if one could simply know the good, one would unswervingly do the good.

On the level of cultural identity, people interpret evil in uniquely ethnic terms, though there is a great deal of overlap in what is considered evil by each group. Though every human group interprets evil uniquely, and though each culture's understanding of evil has evolved over time in step with the evolving self-understandings that provide the markers of similitude within the group, few cultures find the world utterly beneficent and free from evil forces—though some cultures award evil a purifying effect by interpreting it in redemptive ways. The belief that evil abounds is quasi-universal because evil is, for most individuals and most human groups, self-evident. Evil offers empirical evidence of its existence in the suffering of innocents. Theists tend to be those who most readily employ the language and imagery of evil. And yet, paradoxically, evil composes the greatest challenge to their worldview. The theist's worldview rests upon the bedrock of the idea of the existence of an omnipotent, omniscient, and wholly good god. This bedrock is fundamentally challenged by the problem of accounting for the simultaneous existence of things deemed self-evidently evil—the suffering of innocents. If god made the world, knows of the suffering, and has unlimited power, then why does god not design a perfectly just world where innocents do not suffer? If suffering is inevitable in mortal lives, why does he not at least intercede in the lives of suffering innocents to bring them relief?

The extreme view of evil is the metaphysical one held by many theists (from the ancient Greek *meta* as 'above, beyond' and *physis*, 'nature'). According to this view, evil happens as result of *supernatural* forces inhabiting the universe, forces more potent and destructive than mere *natural* energies or powers. Evil in this view is a substance in its own right, waging war against the forces of good in an ongoing cosmic battle, and the battle may be understood to be unfolding toward a climax at some future apocalyptic time, when the god is thought to return to the earth to rule it as a paradisal kingdom in a second "golden age."

This dualistic view of evil has its precedent in Manichaeism, an ancient Persian religion, thought by many scholars to be the world's oldest revealed religion, and perhaps "the only prophetic religion ever produced by the Aryan race."[1] This belief system is considered a heresy by the Catholic/Orthodox Christian Churches, but the "heretics" claim that the early Christian apostles followed this tradition before it was corrupted by the Churches themselves.[2] There is little doubt that some of the elements of the dualism have been transmitted into Judeo-Christian doctrine (through the influence of the Gnostics, for example), evidenced in the efforts of both to purify their systems of traces of the dualism during late antiquity by denying divine status to the evil other god.

Another metaphysical view of evil is exemplified in the proem of the early philosopher, Empedocles of Akragas (Sicily) of the sixth–fifth century B.C.E. In this early cosmology, evil appears as a fundamental cosmic force named Strife (Ēris) that, with Love (Aphrodite) acts upon the four substantive elements (earth, air, fire and water) to bring all manner of being into existence. In Plato, Plotinus, Augustine, and again in the seventeenth century with Spinoza, evil is explained metaphysically, but it is interpreted as a privation in the fullness of being rather than as a separate force or substance in its own right. This understand-

1 R. C. Zaehner, *The Dawn and Twilight of Zoroastrianism* (London: Phoenix Press, 1961), 170.
2 Yuri Stoyanov, *The Other God* (London: Yale University Press, 2000), xi.

ing posits a great chain of being with the god at the helm of the greatest variety possible. Since it is better to be than not to be, being is associated with goodness. So the god is more good the more he creates the fullest possible spectrum of creation. The fullness necessitates differences, but the differences too partake of perfection. A good god lets all things be the best they can be, so the less good are morally limited, not by some simple whim of free will, but by the restrictions inherent in their mortal matter. This view amounts to a kind of determinism that is powerfully tolerant of moral limitation, because those limits are built into the composition of Being.

In monotheistic belief systems, the god must be called upon to give explanation to the existence of bad things, so the nature of the god is necessarily ambiguous, one of his faces being evil, the other benevolent. Certainly, this is true of the nature of deity in the earliest perceptions of human communities. Early Hebrew texts that present the god as jealous and judgmental echo this primal understanding. The god with the dark face shows up in Judeo-Christian myths like the Book of Job and the story of Abraham. Sometimes, the dark face is explained as redemptive, the god's kindness in disguise. In Simone Weil and Emmanuel Levinas, we find late examples of this notion of salvational evil.

I have said that evil poses a logical problem for monotheists. The belief in an all-powerful and all-knowing divine overseer of unlimited compassion and goodness must answer the challenge of why humans suffer when a loving god could, and intuitively should, eliminate that suffering, at least in the case of innocents. In his effort to underscore this problem, Emmanuel Levinas has replaced Leibniz's famed ontological question, "Why is there something rather than nothing?" with the slipperier query: "Why is there evil rather than good?"[1] Leibniz's question affirms Aristotle's declaration of the philosophical primacy of metaphysics but Levinas challenges the philosophical focus of both thinkers by affirming the primacy of ethics: for a world that has seen Holocaust, "ethics is first philosophy," Levinas insists.

It is important to note that, while philosophers and theologians are troubled by the logical and ethical paradoxes plaguing

1 See "Transcendence and Evil" in *Collected Philosophical Papers*, (Dordrecht, Netherlands: Kluwer Academic Publishers, 1987), 175-186.

conceptions of the god and his dark twin, rarely are religious believers stumped by these difficulties. The advantage of a belief system founded on faith and grounded in supernatural, transcendent power is that the paradoxes of that logical system do not challenge but provide evidence to the believer of the fathomless power of the deity. The believer simply leaves the mystery of evil to the infinite wisdom of the god.

Another way of understanding evil is psychologically. Here, evil is seen as a feature of the human *psyche* itself. In Plato, the ambiguities of soul are investigated from many angles. Soul can be understood as having many parts, and evil happens when reason loses control over dangerous passions and appetites. Where Plato presents soul as simple, as a divine spark, ever-moving, ever-changing, the human soul is distinguished from the gods by the latter's being constantly nourished by heavenly excellence. Beauty, temperance, and justice are ethereal realities, and humans do not visit the heavens easily or regularly. The problem is identified by Plato in the *Phaedrus*: when they attempt to rise above the mundane and mirror heavenly perfections, the quality of *phthonos* (all evil qualities spawned by competitiveness are rolled into one word here—greed, envy, competitivism, covetousness, jealousy, greed, malice) causes the aspirants to grapple and struggle against one other, rather than work in unison to ascend the moral heights, as do Plato's orderly gods. Thus do human souls crush and stomp each other's wings and ultimately most fall from the heavens, foregoing the feast of Being that would nourish their higher instincts and place them alongside their divine mentors.

Evil is psychological where it is the result of wayward qualities in the psyche. One might be tempted to equate this with the geneticist's explanation for evil. Genetics holds that evil agency is caused by dispositions toward aggressiveness embedded instinctively in the human species. The most extreme of this view is a biological determinism, where evil is understood as inescapable, predetermined in the genetic make-up of the agent; however, few geneticists hold this extreme view. Most seem to give equal, if not greater, power to the environment in offering the experiential setting for certain (good or evil) dispositions to develop rather than others. Steven Pinker seems to be one of the very rare scientists still claiming that human beings are largely genetically predetermined, our (more and less) nurturing environments having little to do with the kind of people we ultimately become.[1]

The language of evil is seductive and satisfying, especially to people who are suffering and cannot understand their lot. Terms other than evil may be used to describe the bad things that befall people—natural disaster, random catastrophe, a stroke of ill fortune, the tragic element of an otherwise good existence—but there is a measure of existential satisfaction in the use of the terminology of evil. When one is being plagued by very bad things, the term "evil" feeds one's sense of righteous indignation at finding oneself the victim of misfortune.

Many people reserve the term evil for speaking of bad things that are not simple random acts of nature but purposeful acts of a perpetrator. When people deliberately and knowingly cause harm to innocent sentient beings, no term seems to capture the spirit, the meaning, or the intention of the offended one as the term "evil" does. Since I have begun my philosophical investigation of this term, I have discovered that scholarly audiences often express deep concern at the suggestion that this term be retired from use; they argue that no other term seems to do linguistic justice to the seriousness of some events or to the willful moral bankruptcy of some perpetrators.

The concept of evil is attended by a rich vocabulary. This richness may be explained by the fact that there exists such a wide variance in perceptions of evil from place to place and from time to time, from tradition to tradition, and from language to language, and because these traditions, languages, and perceptions admit of dramatic transformations, adaptations, and mutations, and an abundance of additions and omissions within each of these evolving forms, along each of the trajectories of flow of this evolving term.

In the English language, we speak of evil in a great variety of manifestations: sin, impiety, vice, malevolence, cruelty, immorality, criminality, pathology, abomination. Many of the terms employed to denote evil betray the anthropological origins of

1 Steven Pinker. *The Blank Slate*. (Cambridge: Harvard University Press, 2003).

the notion in the ritual life of early human communities, naming the earliest wrongs that were blamed for communal disruptions and came to be regulated through a culture's prescriptions and prohibitions. Incest, fratricide, patricide, cannibalism are examples of archaic notions of evil construed early as extremely problematic because crimes against the gods. Violation of these taboos did not remain with the offender alone but elicited divine vengeance in pollutions that could stalk families for generations (witness Oedipus and the ill fate of each of his children). In the worst cases, these gravest crimes could invite divine retribution against the entire community, in plagues, floods, feuds and other misfortunes. In short, the archaic worldview deemed blameworthy, for individual infractions of moral code, the family and the extended community of which the offender is a part. The offender's acts threatened the welfare of family and friends and disrupted the connection between the community and their ancestors and gods.

The words people choose in speaking about bad things and bad people tell us more about their group than about the group, person, or event being described. The term's attendant vocabulary expresses accepted metaphysical assumptions, moral prejudices, and an orientation toward the world (as threatening or homely). A people's attendant vocabulary of evil reveals whether their cultural group understands the bad things that befall people as breaching divine ordinance (sin, abomination), as a violation of social custom (disgrace, shame, dishonor), as a mistaken, wayward blunder (moral error, mistake) or as a malevolent, purposeful deed of twisted desire (corruption, depravity, cruelty).

The word "evil" comes to us from the Middle English *evel* or *evill*, from the AngloSaxon *yfel*. These words originally denote the possession of bad moral qualities (wickedness, corruption, sinfulness, or badness) and signify the propensity to render bad effects on others in proximity (whether through design, ignorance, or ill luck). Evil is the descriptor attached to persons or things seen to cause pain or misery, to be injurious or threatening injury, or to bring misfortune to its victims.

Ironically, the term "devil," the name religionists often attach to personifications of evil, descends from a more positive history. From the ancient Greek *daimon* or *daemon*, a demon was originally understood to be a median figure, a messenger, arbiter, or facilitator between human beings and the gods, mediators connecting the disparate ontological realms. In ancient myth and philosophy, demons were benevolent mediators, effecting communion among humans and gods. In the earliest Greek tales describing the advent of human beings, the first of the five races of human beings were so peaceful and harmonious that when, after long and happy lives, they passed from their mortal flesh, the gods pronounced them daemons to guide and watch over later, more troublesome mortal races.

In archaic philosophical writings, daemon was also employed to signify a person's unique genius (in a certain art), or, used in a less personal way, the term denoted the moral aspect of the human being. One of the great innovations of Plato's *Phaedo* was his employment of the term *psyche* as a replacement for the older term daemon in speaking of the moral aspect of the person, while yet maintaining the personal aspect of personality or individuality as well. The necessity for this move is clear when we remember that one of Plato's overriding purposes in his early writing was to establish the continuance, not of the soul *per se* in its general status of immortal breath of life (from *pneuma*), but to save from extinction the very personal and unique soul of the beloved Socrates. Without this curious amalgamation of *psyche* with its *daemonic* aspects intact, Plato indeed would have fallen prey to Gregory Vlastos' famed critique in "The Paradox of Socrates."[1] In the hands of the Christian Church, the term demon lost its divine linguistic linkage and its mediational aspect and instead became disruptive, disconnecting, purveyors of strife, serving forces of darkness rather than human interests or the gods.

In *The Devil*, Jeffrey B. Russell opens his historical treatment of personifications of evil with a secularized definition of evil that sets aside the metaphysical baggage generally attached to the terms "evil" and its attendant derivatives. Russell defines evil as "the infliction of pain upon sentient beings," adding later, "hurt deliberately inflicted."[2] The term "evil" employed in this secular-

---

1 Gregory Vlastos, *The Philosophy of Socrates* (New York: Anchor Books, 1971), 1-21.
2 Jeffrey B. Russell, *The Devil*, (Ithaca, N.Y.: Cornell University Press, 1977),

ized vein echoes Aristotle's notion of cruelty, as a form of human wickedness distinguishable from (mere) violence and from unfortunate acts of nature (including animal aggressions) by the explicitly rational aspect of the act, that is, by the intention invested in the agent.[1] This (prior) reflective, deliberative feature narrows the scope of the concept, restricting the use of the term "evil" to an *explicitly* human range of activity, as the work of a rational animal. Only a human being, with its peculiarly rational component fully functional, can commit the "calculated acts of outrage" that compose the evil Aristotle condemns as cruel.

Russell's definition of evil not only exculpates the gods or devils of religious belief for the violence effected by human agents, but it avoids the essentialist claims of the view of evil as monstrous or subhuman. It draws attention to the undesirable nature of the act, and thus counsels rational deliberation for better decision-making, rather than seating evil as a substance embedded in the ontological nature of the agent. Russell's definition affirms evil as explicitly *human*. Human beings can effect bad actions. Therefore human beings can also avoid them.

Evil is often categorized according to the explanatory goal of the discipline engaged in its investigation. Experts from the various respective disciplines speak of social evils, political evils, economic evils, the evils of crimes against humanity, and the evils of aggression. Often the unique form of evil named "genocide" is isolated for analysis as an idiosyncratic evil that demands special examination. People speak of evil families (the Barker Gang) and "communities of evil" (Jamestown). Geneticists locate evil in the flesh where there exists little hope for its healing. Psychologists locate evil in the diseased mind where past traumas have carved out devious paths of understanding, theoretically correctable through analytic self-discovery. Religious anthropologists and cultural critics find the source of evil in the logic of belief systems; political analysts locate it in the dysfunctions of power within the state. In general, sociological accounts find individual acts embedded in social structures; for

---

11 and 17.
1 Aristotle is quoted in A. Caputo et al, "Understanding and Experiences of Cruelty: An Exploratory Report" in *The Journal of Social Psychology* 140(5), 649-660, Part 1.

them, evil is to be understood within the logic and by the terms of those structures. Thus, there can be no absolute evil in sociological accounting.

The study of evil takes the greatest space in the works of theologians, but philosophers, from Plato to Plotinus to Spinoza, who meditate copiously upon the excellence of Being, tend to leave evil as the unspoken other, the unarticulated underside of the Good. Examples of this weak definition of evil abound in ancient philosophy. For Socrates, Plato, and Aristotle, to know the good is to do the good. All people seek happiness, and happiness is fullest when one seeks after the right kind of goods. In the *Euthydemus*, where Socrates and Clinias investigate the goods that give happiness, Socrates argues that none of the things that we call good in general parlance (health, wealth, and power) are good in themselves; they only become authentically good through right use. Socrates' argument prefigures Epicurus' painstaking calibrations of good and evil as pleasure and pain: cake is good, "used" a piece at a time, but "misuse" in the form of eating the whole cake results in the "evil" of a stomach ache.

Socrates and Clinias' exploration concludes in the discovery that, without the virtues of intelligence and wisdom, the "neutral goods"—wealth, health, and good looks are their examples—bring nothing but misery. "If ignorance leads them, they are greater evils than their opposites, inasmuch as they are more able to serve the leader which is evil."[1] Significant here is the fact that beauty, the crucial good of the *Phaedrus* that brings wanton lovers to their reverent knees, is included in the list of neutral goods in the *Euthydemus* argument. Beauty, wealth, and even good health are proposed in the latter dialogue as morally neutral, useless for edification of the soul, and gain moral value only when put to "good use" by those with knowledge of to use things wisely.

Evil results, at least in part, from the improper use of things and from ignorance about what constitutes best uses. Socrates, the know-nothing, understands the difficulty of acquiring the virtue of right usage of things, since right usage issues from right knowledge and wisdom is a property Socrates reserves

---

1 Plato, *Euthydemus* 281b-d.

for the gods alone. Many of us, by Socrates' definition, are likely to fall prey to the ignorance of evil even if we wish desperately to do good. Indeed much harm can come to us and others where we believe we know what we do not know and act rashly. Aristotle recommends a "golden mean" ethos, to replace the Platonic notion of formal excellences that admit of extremes. Where Plato would see evil as a penury of excellence, Aristotle would hold too much courage as foolhardy; too much liberality self-impoverishing.

Robust definitions of evil are rare in the history of philosophy. Even the most pessimistic philosophers who expect the worst from human beings avoid robust ontological definitions of evil, deeming that political and legal systems, carefully constructed, will suffice to keep evil at bay. Thomas Hobbes posits all men engaged in a "war of all against all" but a strong monarch (Leviathan) or a social contract can pacify them and keep them from a life otherwise "solitary, poore, nasty, brutish, and short."[1]

There are many sound reasons for the penury of explicit and robust philosophical attention to the problem of evil. One important reason is that evil does not make for pleasant rumination. Philosophy, as a discipline of study, attracts few enough followers into its painfully convoluted halls, and there is little doubt that it would attract even fewer if it were not for philosophy's escapist dimension that permits thinkers to flee the mundane horrors of history and ascend the lofty heights of abstraction. Wonder, says Socrates, brings a person to philosophy, where a thinker can soar above the dark human cave and, with the gods, feed upon the excellences of Truth and Justice and Beauty.[2] Wonder's dark sister, suffering, can offer an equally demanding philosophical challenge, but, as its questions focus upon much darker objects, they are less seductive to the inquirer.

There exist other more practical reasons for the penury of scholarly interest in the subject of evil. For the scholar to investigate evil, she must first of all trust that something clear is being asked, that evil can be defined with clarity and distinctness. Evil is precisely the term we attach to things we do not understand. Evil is, by many people's definitions, the irrational inexplicable,

1 Thomas Hobbes, *Leviathan*, xiii.1-2
2 Plato. *Theaetetus* 173d & ff.

beyond reasonable inquiry. To investigate evil is to look for reason in something that is by definition unreasonable. Research
becomes senseless, in the special case of evil, because evil is precisely that which is impervious to rational investigation. Monstrous acts don't have reasons; extreme destructiveness is meaningless. To close the investigation into suffering, one need only
assert: they did it because they are evil.

Furthermore, the inquirer into evil, in her attempt to understand horrifying events and their perpetrators, must be ready to
defend her investigation as an evil kind of inquiry. Such investigation, because it challenges the irrationality assumption, risks
offending the victims of radical violences. The idea of investi-
gating reasons for evil undermines the meaningfulness of the
term—for many people evil is *by definition* the unreasonable, as-
cribable only to the madness of perpetrators. Undermining the
meaningfulness of the radical terms victims employ to describe
their situations may be taken by some as an attempt to justify
what their perpetrators have done. Thus investigations into evil
understandably will be offensive to many victims and their loved
ones.

Finally, scholars avoid the investigation of evil because they
aspire to objectivity in their studies. Maintaining the objective
distance thought necessary to an unbiased analytic account can
be daunting, if not impossible, in the case of the most horrifying
events. Socrates tells in the *Theaetetus* that the philosopher gains a
clearer vision of things by climbing above the world and looking
upon things from a thoughtful unattached distance.[1] However,
it is very difficult to maintain a lofty distance when contemplat-
ing the worst events still occurring daily in many parts of the
globe—mass rape, the bayoneting of babies, the humiliations
of prisoners of war, the senseless "collateral damage" of modern
techno-wars, or the brutal slaughter of genocidal projects.

Evil is thus a difficult topic to undertake in scholarly analysis. However, despite the difficulties and dangers, there is good
reason to recommend such analysis. I have been convinced of one
thing through the course of my work as a violence scholar: that
the act of identifying evil and illuminating its location—what

---

1 Ibid.

I name the "moralizing gesture"—composes an ethically pre-carious enterprise. Philosophy counsels *self-*examination for the sake of moral edification. Moralizations in regard of the moral failure of *others* eclipse one's own moral failures, frustrate toler-ance of difference, and grant to the moralizer a dangerous sense of moral elevation to the moralizer. Focus on the failings of other people can serve to legitimate violence against those people. Lo-cating evil in others is a critical step on the way to the practice of things generally deemed evil—the harming of sentient beings.

Much harm has been done in the world, and continues to be done, with the excuse of battling evil. The Crusades had their evil infidels; the Inquisition their demons and witches; Hitler de-monized the Jews, gypsies, Slavs, the handicapped, communists, and other "parasites" feeding off the healthy and noble German *volk*; Rwandan *génocidaires* had their Tutsi "cockroaches"; Zion-ists have their anti-Semitic suicidal terrorists; George W. Bush has his "axis of evil"; General Hillier has his "detestable scum-bags." Everyone who is killing someone somewhere in the world today claims to be defending the innocent home group against a foreign and threatening "evil."

When people come to view *as evil* the people, acts, and events that they witness, they feel justified—and indeed at times com-pelled—to take up the very actions they demonize in others. To understand how this performative contradiction occurs, it is necessary to inquire into the historical frameworks of the lifeworld, the logical and moral parameters that give rise to a people's perceptions of good and evil. We will need to locate where, and to what extent, justifications for evil are embedded in the self-understandings, socio-political assumptions, codes of ethics, and lofty ideals that people employ to inform their moral choices.

Socrates recommends self-examination as the moral curative for evils of the soul, but most people have enormous difficulty seeing the moral fault-lines in their own behaviors, belief sys-tems, traditions, and cultural practices. The paradox of the "in-nocence of evil" is born out in most people's understandings of their own violent actions. Aristotle states: people are bad judges in their own case (*Politics* 1280a15-16). Most people seem to in-tend well for their neighbors and would choose to do the right thing if they could figure out just what that thing is.

To engage in a scholarly discourse about evil is to take up a problematic language, with all its historical, epistemological, and metaphysical baggage. It means to participate in a narration that has itself proven the cause of a great deal of harm in the world. To speak of evil is to place oneself within a tradition that grants the reality of its subject—the reality that evil things and evil people do exist, that we may know them, describe them, analyze them, come to recognize them, and take up scholarly discourse in regard of them. Can we talk about what is experienced as evil without granting reality to evil? Since much harm is done in the world in the name of wiping out evil, does this risky investigation promote further evil rather than help to improve the world?

To participate in the language and logical explication of evil is to enter a history that has itself effected a great deal of harm against sentient beings. On the other hand, to fail to engage *some* things as evil seems equally undesirable, since the denial that evil does occur challenges and undermines the victim experience of suffering and degradation. Thus, a merely scholarly elaboration of the notion of evil must chart an exceedingly delicate route that navigates between a discerning appreciation of victim suffering and the moralizing baggage that attends the history of evil.

The reader will find in the coming pages that my scholarly investigations of evil are juxtaposed with, disturbed by, and interrupted by images by the renowned artist Martin Camarata. When I began my dark explorations, Martin and I would spend our afternoons at the old pastry and coffee shop in the idyllic little town of Turlock, California, where we both lived. I would share with him my shocking discoveries; he would return to his studio and artistically engage my strange ramblings. Our collaborations proved invaluable to our separate enterprises, so we decided to merge our creative products and approach our dark subject through a collaboration between his images and my words.

Artistic image can undercut scholarly discourse and disarm the stark logic of identity, injecting ambiguity into the philosopher's ideas, compelling discourse *as* elusive, obscure, and self-contradictory. Art transforms the logical trajectory of the written word, deconstructs, and refashions it. The ambiguousness created by the meeting of image and word parallels the anxiety, confusion, and perplexity that typify encounters with evil. Artistic image does not tell us what to think about evil, does not impose unequivocal meaning upon that experience, but grants a stage for its ambiguous play and display. Art cannot tell us what to think because the moment a work of art emerges as a phenomenon of perception, it has already escaped the meanings intended by its creator and reached out to its observers in forms radically unique to each. The work of art becomes a theater where our deepest joys, sorrows, and fears are played out, a scaffold for our cognitive pretensions, and a slaughterhouse for the gutting of our clear and distinct ideas.

This project, in staging the meeting of artistic image and philosophical language on the dark and elusive subject of evil, offers a second-level stage, a view from the balcony of the theater, as it were. Through the interplay of image with word, the artist and the philosopher here attempt not simply to re-trace and re-present ideas of evil as they arise in their archaic origins, evolve through the twists and turns of religious discourse in the Judeo-Christian tradition, and find pragmatic application in political usage in modern states. The artist and the philosopher seek to open for the reader new higher-level avenues for thought. As the various aspects of evil unfold from pantheism to dualism to monism, from profligate gods to pristine, from religious worldview to the secular sacred, so too does a theater of cruelty unfurl that reveals evil as a fundamental and integral feature of what is universally cherished as human "civilization."

Our project closes with artistic and philosophical suggestions of for overcoming evil, opening possibilities for working at the margins of our "civilized" lifeworld to disarm the dangerous structure of identity work and its moralizing mechanisms. The words and images in this final chapter are offered as an opportunity to rethink and dislodge the aspects of self- and moral-understanding that promote and legitimate violence against different others. They offer hope for the disarming of the over-serious fascinations with autonomy, freedom, and sovereignty that attend Western notions of subjectivity.

The core message of this work is that there exists a direct relationship, in all cultures, in all religions, and in all political ideologies, between the way people conceive of (conceptualize) evil and the way they conceive (give birth to) evil. When they see evil as emanating from corrupt religious beliefs, people may support armed crusades to wipe out the infidels. When people understand evil as the work of morally backward cultures, they cannot see the short-term possibility for speeding up the processes of evolution so may opt for slavery, oppression, or slaughter as cures for the "primitives." Where a people harbor poignant social memories of their culture's past victimization, oppression, or dishonor or where they understand their cultural identity in terms of historical grandeur now lost, they may locate evil in the current cultural or national populations of their historical enemies rather than in historical persons long dead.

On the other hand, when people see ignorance as causing the problems they encounter in their worlds, they tend to favor enlightened social policies that offer supports—educational and other benefits—to cure the ills in their nations and across the globe. Where they understand poverty as the root of evil, they will tend to support progressive policies of state welfare, school meal programs, socialized medicine, inner-city youth support programs, and the like, that cast safety nets around the base of society to buttress potential offenders before they fall into evil.

Evil and its many derivative terms are highly seductive and satisfying. When we use these terms to refer to the things and people that appall us, there is a deep sense that we have got it right. Other, less demonizing terms simply fail to capture the profound sense of indignation we wish to attach to the worst people and events: to call the Holocaust an unfortunate event or General Idi Amin Dada a bad man misses the mark of our disdain for them. We need to be aware, however, that as gratifying as extreme moralizing language and imagery may feel, they can come at a high moral cost.

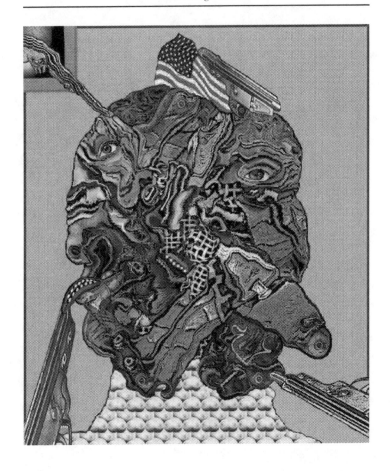

CHAPTER ONE. THE PHENOMENON OF EVIL

Evil is almost exclusively the language of victims, though it may be used by sympathetic bystanders to signal their empathy with the victim. It is an extreme term that circumvents meaningful content and goes straight to the emotional aspect of the event. Evil is a perception before it is a meaningful descriptor: it voices the moral outrage that people feel (or that we feel people ought to feel) when they are treated unfairly. I qualify the former statement with the prescriptive second-level perception "that we feel people ought to feel" because of the fact that we sense that deeply objectionable acts *require* our moral outrage, though in fact cruel and barbaric treatment can often be dispassionately accepted by both victims and observers if they believe the treatment to be deserved by the recipient or performed by the perpetrator without malice. The term evil will be applied to the event, as well as the perpetrator of the event, only where two factors are present. The victim must be sympathetically viewed as undeserving of the treatment *and* the perpetrator must be seen as intending the suffering out of sheer delight in inflicting suffering or utter apathy about another's suffering.

Evil can thus be said to reside in the category of perception. It is a phenomenon that arises only in relation to unjust desserts. Victims and victim sympathizers do not raise the *question* of evil. That is to say, evil is not a question for them because it offers its own self-evidence. The experience of evil, as opposed to the experiences of misfortune, natural calamity, or simple hardship, is a dimension of human experience that needs no further verification; it carries within its experience its self-authentication. That is, victims or sympathetic observers simply *find evil* in their field of experience; they do not find a questionable event, which they consider rationally and then declare to fall into the category of evil things. They simply find evil things or people *as evil*. Evil is an experience, viewed from the vantage point of the victim.

I have said that the language of evil is the language of the victim, and through empathetic sensibility, the language of the sympathetic bystander. However, there are several aspects of the experience of evil that tend to be perceived differentially by victim and bystander. First, the victim perception of evil is often accompanied by the sense of feeling specially targeted by a willing perpetrator for the ill treatment. Though random bad things happen to undeserving people in every society, when an evil thing happens *to me* the phenomenon is generally accompanied by a sense of me as targeted. It motivates the reaction: *Why me?* The question may not be directed to the perpetrator per se, so much as the universe in general for sorting out destiny in this cruel way. Or God's goodness or sense of justice may be called into question, if the victim is a believer, though believers usually have many and various explanations ready at hand for excusing God's moral failures.

I have said that evil is the language and experience of victims and victim sympathizers, a phenomenon that people "find," rather than a mere invention the human mind purposely creates or a judgment imposed upon reality. Evil *comes to appearance* manifest in a *lived experience*. To say that people discover evil as an existent aspect of their world is different from claiming an objective empirical proof of the existence of evil. To say that evil is an aspect of victim experience is not to make a truth claim for or against the existence of evil. Rather, phenomenological expressions simply admit a fact to which experience testifies every day—nothing meaningful presents itself to understanding independent of a meaning context. Phenomenology recognizes that meaning interpretation is not a voluntary condition willfully imposed upon the brute facts that sum up to give us "world."

Rather, things arise as meaningful phenomena of a world because interpretive possibility serves up a sense of coherent reality—world, cosmos—rather than chaos.

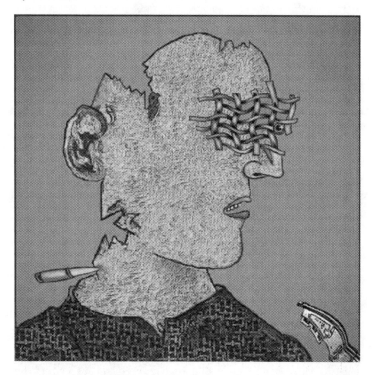

My choice of phenomenological expression of the experience
of evil ("people find evil") over more confident "objective" truth
claims is meant to accomplish two objectives. On the one hand,
phenomenological inquiry takes very seriously the authenticity
of the "reality" as experienced by the human subject. As well,
my use of the phenomenological approach here expresses the
deep suspicion, shared by many philosophers of the postmodern era, of science's pretensions to be the impartial authority on
truth. Phenomenology undercuts the modernist confidence in
rationality as the sole determinant and guarantor of truth and
science as offering an "objective" account of the absolute reality
of everything. Jacques Derrida captures this suspicion with his
famed phrase, "There is nothing outside the text" (*Il n'y a pas de*

hors-text).[1]

In the tradition of Edmund Husserl and G.W.F. Hegel, Derrida's cryptic phrase demonstrates a phenomenological fact—that even the most supposedly "objective" scientist accesses her sense of world, her reality, from the perspective of a human subject. Outside the laws of physics, all scientific truth, however universally agreed upon, amounts to no more than a human subjective experience of reality; all human truth is subjective truth. Or, rather, the distinction between subjective (read: mythical, religious, emotional, individual) and objective (read: scientific, rational, universal) reality is a false dichotomy. Most scientists rebel at this claim, since it offends the sanctity of the edifice of knowledge which grounds their vocational activity and gives meaning to their lives and work. However, rendering all truth claims as interpretive activity, as text, does not mean that truth is impossible. It means that truth is impossible for us to know. It means we must remain humble about our truths and tolerant of others' differing truths, keeping open the question of absolute truth, as do Socrates and other radical skeptics.

This means that we cannot question the truth of the phenomenon of evil, or of any phenomena for that matter. This is why phenomenology does not engage in questions of empirical or representational truth. What is true for a subject is taken to be true, simply and naively, by the phenomenologist. To raise the question of the veracity of experience is to think against the grain of phenomenological study. Edmund Husserl, the father of phenomenology, warns against opposing phenomenological truth to some other more real truth gleaned through the objective attitude of the scientist. Rather, Husserl insists that there is nothing but the phenomenon; subjects have no access to the world except through their experiences of phenomena. This is true of the victim of evil no less than it is true of the scientist. So the phenomenologist puts aside questions of truth or falsity and simply studies naively the subjective experience to see what it can tell us about the way that human lives are lived.

Evil presents a compelling challenge to phenomenological

---

1 Jacques Derrida, "*Structure, Sign and Play in the Discourse of the Human Sciences*," *Critical Theory Since 1965*. H. Adams and L. Searle, eds. (Gainesville, Florida.: Florida State University Press: 1986), 83-94.

study as the study of human experience. This is because the phenomenon of evil has a specific quality that defies the humanness of the experience. For the subject who is also victim, or a bystander sharing the victim perception through empathy, evil is a *human* experience of the *inhumanity* of another *human* being. The phenomenon comes to appearance always already illuminating an *ontological* differential. The evildoer comes to appearance as distinctly another *kind* of being, an other to *human* being. Further, the ontological status of the evil other is ambiguous in its differential relation to the human. On the one hand, the evil thing or person is less than the human, lower on the ontological scale, and since ontological scales compose always morally significant rankings and orderings of beings, lower in moral worth. Concomitantly, however, the evil phenomenon is simultaneously experienced as greater than the human, not limited by the usual constraints against harmdoing that we believe to be hardwired into human beings and something more alien to our reason than human understanding can fathom.

Thus the "greater than/less than" quality inherent in the phenomenon of evil maintains in two capacities: what is evil is generally experienced as both great in potency and great in malevolence. It is the "greater while lesser" (than the human) aspect of the phenomenon that places the phenomenon beyond the pale of human reasoning and that evokes a response of dread and horror. The victim struggles to make sense of the horrifying by associating it with other known horrors, other phenomena that make us feel powerlessness and loathing: disease, contamination, death, rotting corpses, malignancy. Like a cancer masquerading as healthy tissue, the evil phenomenon infects, consumes, undermines, and destroys other healthier beings. Moreover, since evil appears as powerful, and since exercising power is a pleasant experience, the victim further assumes that the perpetrator of evil takes pleasure in, or at least is indifferent to, the suffering he/she/it causes in others.

Phenomena are not timeless; our experiences are historically and socially embedded and determined, as Hegel has demonstrated. Often, our experience evolves over time and the subject comes to see that what at first appeared as true is later contradicted. It is not that the new truth cancels out the old or that the old experience is any less true in hindsight. Rather, the phenomenon evolves to a higher level of truth. This is often the case with phenomena that offer self-evidence of being evil. Ultimately the experience of pronounced potency and malevolence shows itself as grossly exaggerated. The heightened initial response to the phenomenon of evil often gives way to a more measured and rational response as emotions give way to reason. A child comes to see, with the light of day, that the monster in the closet that caused his night terrors is simply the shadow of his hockey shirt. The strange neighbor lurking about in the garden at night loses his fearsomeness when we learn that he has a passion for night-blooming orchids.

Evil is a phenomenological occurrence but it is an experience that comes into being within a certain worldview. That worldview is framed necessarily by fear and horror and ignorance. I can say this because the problem of evil arises in response to fearsome, horrifying things people do not understand. The phenomenon amounts to a very localized experience, because all three of the factors must be present—fear, horror, and ignorance—for evil to appear, but all three qualities exist within the victim-subject and not in the objectified other, the evil one; though fear, horror, and ignorance may maintain in the general atmosphere of the surrounding lifeworld that shapes the victim worldview. A subject's experience is always filtered through a schema of local reality postulates, shaped and shaded by local circumstances and configured by the logic of the "common mental world" of the larger social context, a world uniquely determined by the group's peculiar histories.

Trauma changes individuals and peoples, and it rarely changes them for the better. When a person or a people's peculiar histories include traumatic events, the effects radically alter the way that their futures will be lived and difference will be received. Trauma damages psyches, rendering people fearful and suspicious and making their world appear threatening and hostile. The mythological worldview populated by clear and distinct objects that are unambiguously either good or evil can help to sort out the chaos of victim lives in the aftermath of horrors. Thus, once a person or people have known evil, they may readily find it again. We should not be surprised to find the language of evil in the employ of people who have suffered greatly. For Jews in a post-Holocaust world, for Palestinians in their barbed-wire compounds, for Rwandan or Cambodian villagers, and for Americans in a post 9/11/01 world, evil lurks everywhere.

Yet, curiously, we find the language of evil on both sides of many tragedies, even conflicts where the perpetrator and victim seem so clearly demarcated, where the identity of the bad guy seems beyond contention. Adolf Hitler had his mythology of evil; Richard Koenigsberg counts hundreds of instances where Hitler refers to the Jews in terms of a dangerous infection seeking to destroy the noble German *volk*.[1] The use of the language of evil by obvious perpetrators not only highlights a crucial phenomenon about the connection between suffering and evil—the violent-proneness of victim populations. The language of evil by perpetrators raises a troubling question: do we purge people from our midst because they are evil, or do we name them evil so we can purge them? Hitler said: *If the Jews had not existed, we would have had to invent them.*

Perpetrators often demonize their victims before they commit their atrocities. So too do military training programs vilify their intended victims before sending their troops out to kill. Prior demonization of victims serves several important purposes for perpetrators. It helps to qualm the natural aversion that people generally share at the prospect of killing one of their own kind. Studies, such as Christopher Browning's *Ordinary Men*, show that the human body often revolts when the mind is willing to join in a killing spree, making executions impossible.[2] Executioners may vomit, their bodies may shake uncontrollably, and they sometimes pass out cold at the prospect of killing another human being. If commanders can convince their killer squadrons that the proposed victims are less than human, the troops have a better stomach for the dirty deeds they must perform. Furthermore, those brutal acts executioners and military personnel are asked to perform are under normal conditions deemed evil, but those same acts are morally purified by

---

1 Richard Koenigsberg, *Hitler's Ideology: A Study in Psychoanalytic Sociology* (New York: Library of Social Science, 1975).
2 Christopher R. Browning, *Ordinary Men: Reserve Police Battalion 101 and the Final Solution in Poland* (New York: Harper Perennial, 1998), 128.

the claim that the victim population is evil. The natural aversion to killing can be overcome and the killer morally elevated by the act of killing, so killing campaigns will prove more successful. Somehow the acts that are commonly deemed evil must be reconciled with the perpetrators' self-images that they are good people performing an important function for humankind. The language and imagery of evil helps in this reconciliation.

The fact that perpetrators often apply the language of evil in its various forms when talking about their victims, while rarely using it to describe their own actions—actions they would just as readily deem evil in others—demonstrates a general human capacity: the tendency to find ready fault in others while readily downplaying the moral dimension of our own actions. While the phenomenological experience of evil serves up perpetrators as powerful and malevolent, a phenomenological shift occurs when viewing our own actions. We tend to view our own actions much more innocently. This shift can permit the most morally-sensitive to commit violence against others without the moral clarity they usually enjoy. This fact inclines me toward a disquieting theory: there may not exist the great gap that we conveniently insert in our minds between perpetrators and victims.

The theory I am advancing here resonates with the important—if scandalous—work of French philosopher Georges Bataille. Certainly Bataille seems to fit within a work that considers evil. The "depraved ravings" of this "bad poet" express a morbid and revolting fascination for sexual excesses, horrifying tortures, and undesirable body parts and acts. Cruel and violent phenomena punctuate the pages of his writings, which are more like depraved confessions than philosophy. Bataille seems to know evil, but can he contribute to a scholarly discussion that seeks to reduce the evils of the human world?

Bataille's "bad poetics," like the artist's provocative images, accomplish a sleight of hand that could not be accomplished alone by the reasonable calculations of a philosophical treatise, which must operate within the system of signs and symbols that constitute scholarly discourse and issue in a common mental world. Scholarly discourse must necessarily practice the logic and language that underpin dominating systems of meaning.

Bataille's writing is self-sacrificial. It constitutes a painful struggle where meanings fail and sense becomes nonsense. Bataille enacts, in writing, a dissolution of logical reasoning, a labored birth of absurdity that does not explain or dictate truth. Bataille opens the reader's possibilities for interpretation outside the dominant postulates of reality, by revealing the unthinkable—that the ape's anus is as beautiful as it is obscene. His fascination with transgression seeks to unmask a common fragility in the steadfastness of our own moral boundaries. His "decadent fantasies" expose the extreme possibility of human being, a possibility that our purifying logic works so desperately to conceal—the possibility that, at the core of human desire—the desire shared by *all* human beings—there lurks the very monster who, in the conscious moralizing life, we so starkly condemn in others. Bataille reveals the murderousness that founds all human community when he exposes the darker dreams that rage in the human breast.

In his article "Reflections on the Executioner and the Victim," a treatment of David Rousset's *Les Jours de notre mort*, Bataille collapses the comfortable categories of victim and executioner that help us to make sense of the world and to expiate our implication in worldly atrocities. Bataille notes, with Rousset, not the common dignity of humanity but the common "ignobility" of the victim and his executioner, the common moral frailty of the best and the worst of our species.[1] Bataille disrupts the comfortable polar identities that grant us purification from evil. In collapsing the neat dichotomy of innocence and cruelty, Bataille shakes our common mental world. We are all potentially victims, and equally potentially executioners of our neighbors. All, for Bataille, are mutually bound in a common "decomposition of being." Distinctions in the human community of victim–perpetrators can be made only in terms of the rhythm by which our moral decomposition proceeds: the great human being decomposes more slowly, but, ultimately, all are certain of collapse.

Bataille continues this scandalous logic: it is not simply that each person succumbs to moral degradation under extremities

---

1 Georges Bataille, "Reflections on the Executioner and the Victim," *Yale French Studies. Literature and the Ethical Question.* Number 79. Claire Nouvet, ed. (New Haven, Conn.: Yale University Press. 1991), 15-19.

of suffering and humiliation (as Primo Levi has exposed in his seminal *The Drowned and the Saved*).[1] Of course, extremes of abjection open onto "a universe of suffering, of baseness and of stench" that swallows each at a greater or lesser pace, but, ultimately swallows all. Certainly sufferings—say, from sickness or accidents of fate—can degrade one morally, but can also be purifying and morally enlightening, gathering fellow sufferers in a common bond that seeks to better the world. Bataille asserts:

> A world in which many individuals would suffer great pain but in which the common goal was to fight pain would be soothing. A world of suffering finds its reasons. In such a world, victims have right on their side; they are sanctified by the pains and degradation.[2]

Bataille acknowledges the moral usefulness and the moral dangers of suffering. Quite comprehensible is the sufferer who succumbs to the ways of the system and abuses his companions in suffering, such as Levi's "drowned saved" come to do. Bataille is gesturing toward some darker human potentiality in this essay, a deeper human horror, the horror that resides, not at the core of the sufferer, but at the core of the executioner. The most deeply concealed terror that the victim discovers as she stares into the abyssal face of her torturer is her own reflection. Bataille forces the reader to gaze into that abyss, and in so doing he makes us face up to a common human possibility—that each of us shares, with the torturer, the possibility of evil. Torture, cruelty, and brutality seem inhuman but the evil acts of the torturer compose, for Bataille, the very limits that give meaning to the category of "human." Extreme possibilities delineate identity; cruelty marks out the human *as such*.

Bataille's shocking truth affirms the banality of evil, the potentiality for torture in the best and the worst of us. The most sacred of identity spaces—familial, religious, ethnic, national—shares with the Third Reich, the kingdom of Genghis Khan, with Mao's "Great Leap Forward," and Stalin's Russia, the potential for the senseless rage of the torturer, an entirely human rage that

---

1 Primo Levi, *The Drowned and the Saved*, Raymond Rosenthal, tr. (New York: Vintage Books. 1989).
2 Ibid., 18.

dwells on the cusp of the human condition.

Bataille's "indecent" fantasies mock the claim of most religious and mythical traditions that humans mirror the image of god. By leveling us all, on the deepest level, to the potentially demonic, he undercuts the scapegoat mechanism that people readily apply to their enemies to purify themselves and their violences. Bataille collapses the dichotomy of good and evil, disarming the demonizing gesture that grants killers their stomach for enemy blood. He refuses evil as a contaminating principle of moral disfigurement effected from without upon the human world. He exposes the absurdity of the extant order's dualistic logic as he acts out, with his mutinous writing, a revolution *within* that very order.

Bataille's literary excesses expose a metaphysically rapacious world so fully embellished as to supplant any posited sense of the absurd. His freewheeling carnival of bodily mishap, the torment, the perversions and the orgies defy the claims of the innocent sanctity of existing socio-moral orders. Bataille's excesses of cruelty expose the dark truth of our civilizations: that violence is always already an ineluctable element of all social, economic, and political orders per se. Like the Marquis de Sade, Bataille unveils the cruel underside of the polite human world, exposing that lofty moral ideals and rituals of refined human engagement are fundamental to its cruelty.

Bataille's, as de Sade's, literary spectacles of violence are not meant as mere exploitations of sex and violence, though they are often misread as such. Their scandalous images are designed to open the possibility of alternatively configured relations between human fellows, beyond the coalitions forged by mechanisms of rejection, beyond the easy demonizations of our enemies. His meditations on cruelty illustrate, if outrageously, that while suffering bodies are individual, the readiness to harm others is a collective human feature. The world is a theater of suffering and violence, nurturance and exploitation. Nothing whatsoever fits neatly into the neat categories by which we understand world. To apply Primo Levi's terminology, all is a gray zone.

Recognizing the violent forces that are at work in any culture, recognizing our deepest concealments of our own violent tendencies, recognizing that the more passionately "moral" we are, the more we are enslaved to the demonizing logic, recognizing that the more ordered and "sacred" the system, the more wounding it is likely to be toward the marginalized and the non-belonging—these re-*cognitions* can help us to overcome our tendency to channel chaos onto those who are different or expel it upon foreign bodies. They can help dispel the intractable oversights that purify our violences.

The domain of violence coextends with the over-determined assembly of powers and forces that configure the human world. There exists no purified realm of the good cut loose from the orchestrations of evil. Any order's social terrain is co-extensive with the monstrousness it condemns in its enemies. Ordering systems not only suppress and regulate violence; they comprise it and produce it.[1] Mechanisms of control and organization—Homeland Security offices, police interrogations, armed guards, security checkpoints, military orders, immigration controls—do not simply bar evil others from our polite societies. Prohibitions and regulations increase the fear and sense of powerlessness of every member of the society and promote in otherwise peaceful populations the rage that motivates Bataille's torturers. Rage is manifest in the frantic moralizations that flood the public sphere in Western societies. We witness it in the public hysterias surrounding abortion, pornography, capital punishment, and terrorism. Rage is evidenced in the frenzied denouncements of "axes of evil" and "decadent civilizations." We see it in the over-serious nationalisms, tribalisms, and religious fundamentalisms that flood the globe in the modern era. Guilt or innocence is beside the point in theatricalized condemnations of social enemies. The condemnation of others depends on a sustained and orchestrated refusal to recognize that violence—evil—is not external to, and threatening to infiltrate, our sacred social fabric, but is constitutive of it.

Foreign civilizations are not demonic; the moralizing gesture

---

1 Through this lens, then, social reality is itself guided by an illusion. Ordered systems are nothing short of ideological fantasies, at whose margins the non-belonging play a constitutive role by marking out the crucial agonistic limits in the contested terrain of belonging. Though ordered systems pretend practical and theoretical coherence, they simply suppress the chaos—hide their dead, repress the suffering that offends the modern liberal ethic.

that posits the moral failure of foreigners and grants license to kill them is demonic. The stark fact of the matter is that evil is a rather mundane and common phenomenon, manifesting in a range of everyday experiences across the globe—in famine, flood, ageing, disease, heartbreak and war. As Bataille demonstrates, most evils cannot be separated, let alone purified, from the human condition. Those few evils that can be remedied generally come about as a result of applying inflexible moral distinctions. It is not the evils of corrupt others that render our societies dangerous, but the purifying, demonizing mechanism that clarifies and illuminates the monstrousness of others with a rigorous and absolute clarity.

CHAPTER TWO. EVIL IN THE LOGIC OF THE COSMOS

En arche én ho logos. John 1:1

The words, images, and symbols captured in a people's language tell much about their worldview, what they hold dear
and what they despise, what appears safe and comforting and
what lurks as dangerous, where their gods dwell and where evil
is seen to lurk. This is truer of the words of ancient languages
than of modern, since ancient words tend to be much richer and
broader in meaning than the terms of modern languages whose
demand for scientific exactness has forced a reductionism that
seeks to eliminate ambiguity.

In this chapter, we shall consider an overriding value of the
modern world, the value of order, to determine the origin of this
value in Greek cosmology and its effect on our collective Western consciousness, and we shall question the appropriateness of
this value for fitting us for peaceful coexistence in a democratic
world of endless human difference. We shall see that, contrary
to the comfort this value ostensibly promises to its disciples,
struggling against the troubling flux and change of everyday life,
too great an appreciation for this value can situate human beings for repressive and even violent responses to the vicissitudes
that are the very nature of human existence and the condition of
human life.

1. Love of Order in the Western Tradition

In the ancient Greek language, one of the richest terms is *logos* (λόγος), literally meaning "word" and connecting to the verb *logein* (λόγειν), "to say or tell."[1] True to ancient fashion, the word *logos* denotes meanings far beyond its literal "word," a richness captured in Liddle and Scott's secondary meanings: "that by which the inward thought is expressed" and "the inward thought itself."[2] *Logos* is used to refer to anything the human mind comes up with. It can mean story, tale, argument, a speech or oration, a definition or explanation, reason or rational basis. Beyond an individual person's story or reasoning, however, *logos* refers to a logic or order of reason that expands outward into the society and indeed across the structure of the cosmos.

Logos can stretch beyond the content of individual thought to point toward the stable, dependable aspect of ideas as structured according to a universal reason. The logical aspect of a proposition or a mathematical principle, for example, offers a much more reliable truth than the content of an individual's account of truth.

The distinction between individual thought content and universal reason does not suggest a dichotomy between mythological or religious, faith-based reckoning and scientific ideas. In fact such a distinction makes no sense within the ancient Greek worldview. This fact is visible in the construction of the word for recounting a legend or crafting a tale: *mythologein* (*mythologein*) is formed by the combination of the word to tell (*logein*) and the word for myth (*mythos*). A deeper, more timeless aspect of truth was understood to be contained in mythical tales, rather than myths being thought fantastic stories or fictions, according to the modern distinction. Myths often dealt with beginnings and for the Greeks, beginnings of things contain their deepest truths, albeit in the elusive garb of image and symbol.

Logos is also the word for law, which codes of prescriptions and prohibitions record the people's traditional political and ethical ideas on matters of proper conduct for civilians and

---

1 Liddle and Scott, *An Intermediate Greek-English Lexicon* (Oxford, U.K.: Oxford University Press, 1997), p. 476-477.
2 Ibid.

statesmen. The word comes, with Aristotle, to denote logic, the rigorous laws of language and reason and the rules and regulations that govern the structure of arguments.

Dictionary definitions demonstrate the breadth of meanings encapsulated in ancient words, but the word *logos* is richer than most terms. *Logos* has an import in the ancient Greek worldview that escapes the limits of lexiconic classification. With the Greeks, the "inward thought" aspect of this word overflows its conceptual bounds and evolves into a universal structure of reason and a principle of cosmic harmony that holds the universe in place. Thus *logos* is a force or power much greater than, though reflected in, the contents of human minds. *Logos*—firm, constant, eternal, always true—shows up in the "inner thoughts" of humans but it is not identical with those thoughts. *Logos* is the brilliance that occasionally flickers in human reasoning, the truth, order, or wisdom that represents the best and most reliable in human intelligence. Humans access truth on occasion because the human mind has access to a great force beyond the human brain, the *logos* which flows through, orders, and illuminates all things (to greater and lesser degrees of perfection), and steers them toward truth and right. *Logos* is grander, more respected, more imposing than individual thoughts and reasons; it is Reason itself speaking through human minds in their highest speculations and their most accurate calculations.

Connected with truth and excellence, then, *logos* has deep ethical significance in the ancient worldview. *Logos* is a force embedded in the cosmos, a power that is good and right and just, and that underlies and steers all things toward their best ends. *Logos* is visible in the perfect measure that regulates the daily cycles of the sun, the orbits of the heavenly bodies, and the coming and going of the seasons. *Logos* is the archaic principle embedded in the Greek notion of *cosmos* (κόσμος "order, world, universe, ordered and harmonious whole"); the world makes sense, and the human mind has hope of accessing an occasional truth because *logos* (reason) guides all things rightly.

The ancient Greek worldview posited four divine elements (earth, air, fire and water), personified as gods, as the stuff from which world comes to be made. But multiplicity, for the Greeks, represents an embarrassment of riches, a troubling, messy many-ness. Simplicity is always preferable to multiplicity, for the Greeks, as cosmos is preferable to chaos; the many require a principle of order or reason, a *logos*, to bring them into harmonious balance.

Earliest Greek philosophers seek to unify the four building blocks of existence by naming a primary ruling agent to bring the four into the reasonable harmony that grants cosmos; in Thales (c. 624–546 BCE) and Anaximenes (c. 585–525 BCE), one of the sacred four is assigned the task—water and air, respectively. Anaximander (c. 610–546 BCE) holds that the ordering principle must be greater in reality and different from what is being ordered. He names the ordering principle *apeiron* (from Ancient Greek privative α + πείρος, or *apeiros*, literally "no-passageway" or "no way through"), by which he means a power underlying, empowering, and harmonizing the four, but beyond human comprehension.

Heraclitus (c. 535–475 BCE) agrees that the ordering principle must be more profound and powerful than the elements but refuses that the principle is removed from human understanding. Rather, he asserts that the order of the cosmic whole and the reasonableness of things is guaranteed by reason itself, a power in which humans share when they think and speak, whenever they perform these activities rightly; that is, if they are wise.

The principle of *logos* is most clearly seen in Heraclitus' philosophy. Heraclitus employs the term *logos* to denote the reasoned, ordered constancy that underlies and grounds the infinite flux of earthly existence. Although Heraclitus is best known for his doctrine of flux (*panta rei* or "everything flows"), references to his philosophy in ancient sources make abundantly clear that Heraclitus holds *logos* to compose a deeper reality than the flux. He counsels humans to try to comprehend the underlying coherence in things, a coherence that he identifies as the *logos*, the principle or formula common to all things. He states:

> Of the *Logos* which is as I describe it men always prove to be uncomprehending, both before they have heard it and once they have heard it. For although all things happen according to this Logos, men are like people of no experience, even when they experience

such words and deeds as I explain. . .

(Fr. 1, Sextus *adv. math.* VII, 132.)

> They do not apprehend how being at variance it agrees with itself.

(Fr. 51, Hippolytus *Ref.* IX, 9, 1)

> Therefore it is necessary to follow the common; but although the Logos is common, the many live as though they had a private understanding.

(Fr. 2, Sextus, *adv. math.* VII, 133.)

> The path up and down is the same path.

(Fr. 60, Hippolytus *Ref.* IX, 10, 4)

Logos orders and steers the universe from within, holding the many beings in appropriate and just "measures" (*metra*). A number of fragments imply that both faith and perseverance are required to discover the underlying truth of things and see their common *Logos*.

For Heraclitus, *Logos* represents the unity in things and of things; it comprises the balance in the fluctuating opposites (hot–cold, dry–wet, up–down) that renders cosmos, an ordered whole despite the troubling change and flux. Heraclitus must have recognized that his doctrine of the flux, more scandalous to Greek ears, would compose his greatest legacy. This may explain why he counsels the wisdom of the *logos* over his word in his assertion: *Listening to the logos rather than to me, it is wise to agree that all things are in reality one thing and one thing only* (Fr. 50, Hippolytus *Ref.* IX, 9, I).

Heraclitus' advice is generally ignored, and he continues to be taught in Introductory Philosophy classes as the "philosopher of the flux." However, Kirk and Raven, in their definitive text, *The PreSocratic Philosophers*, conclude their chapter on Heraclitus with the following telling assertion:

> In spite of much obscurity and uncertainty of inter-
> pretation, it does appear that Heraclitus' thought pos-
> sessed a comprehensive unity. . . . Practically all aspects

of the world are explained systematically, in relation to a central discovery—that natural changes of all kinds are regular and balanced, and that the cause of this balance is fire, the common constituent of things that was also termed their *Logos*.[1]

Parmenides (early 5th century BCE), younger contemporary of Heraclitus, writes in conscious opposition to Heraclitus' doctrine of the flux. Going beyond Heraclitus' claim that *logos* underlies all change and multiplicity and holds the universe in harmonious balance, Parmenides insists that change *is not*. Echoing Heraclitus in Fragment 50 (above), Parmenides asserts that talk about and belief in change is simply a human mistake. How does Parmenides, a human being himself, discover this god's-eye truth? Parmenides' didactic poem, *On Nature*, describes a dream in which Parmenides ascends to the heavens to meet "the goddess" who initiates him into secret knowledge about the true nature of reality.

The Proem describes a youthful Parmenides borne heavenward on a chariot attended by maidens of the sun. They guide him on a journey along the highway of Night till they reach the massive Gate of Night and Day, which is barred shut. The key is in the keeping of *Dike* (Justice), but the maidens persuade the god to unlock the gate and let them pass. Onward into the Day the chariot rolls till it arrives at the palace of the goddess, who welcomes and instructs Parmenides in the two ways of knowing: the Way of Truth and the Way of Seeming.

> Come now and I will tell thee—and do not hearken and carry my word away—the only ways of enquiry that can be thought: the one way, *that it is and cannot not be*, is the path of Persuasion, for it attends upon Truth; the other—*that it is not and needs must not be*, that I tell thee is a path altogether unthinkable. For thou couldst not know that which is not, nor utter it; the same thing exists for thinking as for being. That which can be spoken and thought needs must be; for it is possible for it, but not for nothing, to be. One way only is left to be spoken

1 G.S. Kirk and J.E. Raven, *The PreSocratic Philosophers* (Cambridge, U.K.: Cambridge University Press, 1983), p. 212.

of, that it *is*; and on this way are full many signs that *what is* is uncreated and imperishable, for it is entire, immovable, and without end. It *was* not in the past, nor *shall* it be, since it *is* now, all at once, one, continuous; for what creation wilt thou seek for it? how and whence did it grow?

The goddess counsels Parmenides, on an argument grounded in the logic of identity and non-contradiction, that single, immutable, ordered Being is all that exists. Parmenides has taken the logic of the cosmos one step farther than his predecessor. Where multiplicity is illusion and change is overcome, order and harmony no longer require an "underlying" sponsor but *logos* comprises the very being of the One.

The love of *logos*, the ordering principle for the cosmos, is fundamental to the Greek worldview and testifies to the Greek sense of the world as sacred, profoundly ordered, good, and harmonious. Whether posited as the ground for existence, change, and multiplicity, or as the One and all that is, the *logos* is older and more powerful than created things, more real and more reliable than the gods. The Greek assumption that an ordering power, a reason, a *logos*, orders all existence and steers it toward the good grounds the Western understanding of the world. This assumption also undergirds all scientific inquiry in the West. We moderns may imagine that we have outgrown such ideas as a good, just Logos, underlying the flux of multiplicity, but if truth be told, our trust that scientific investigation is a worthwhile pursuit and its conclusions reliable rests upon an assumption very similar to the Greek notion of logos: we trust that the universe is reasonable, can be understood, and makes sense, because it is governed by natural laws that are constant, immutable, and logical.[1]

2. Evil in the Unreason of Humans

The love of *logos*, or reasoned, harmonious order is a feature fundamental to the Greek worldview. The distinguishing features of the *logos*—order, reason, stability, simplicity, change-

1 Kirk & Raven, *The PreSocratic Philosophers* (Cambridge: Cambridge University Press, 2002), 245.

lessness—are seen as the most desirable qualities to which all people and things should aspire. Plato has Socrates recommend to the highest souls the study and imitation of the heavens, with their constant cycles and their fixed seasons.[1] Where order, reason and stability are beloved, chaos, ignorance, and change are reviled. Evil, in the ancient world as in the modern West, is associated with that which reason (*logos*) cannot control, what escapes the limits of the law (*logos*), what ruptures the comfortable boundaries of definition (*logos*)—the limitless, the immeasurable, the ungraspable, the chaotic.

In the Greek mind, overstepping one's limits is the worst human crime, causing hardship to the human world and offense to the gods. *Hybris* is the name the Greeks give to that state of overblown pride or arrogance that is evident in human beings who overstep their rightful measure and forget their proper place in the whole of things. Perhaps the best (and most humorous) example of *hybris* is the myth that Plato places in the mouth of the comic poet Aristophanes in the dialogue *Symposium*. The tale opens with Aristophanes' hilarious description of an original human state. The poet tells that humans were:

> globular in shape, with rounded back and sides, four arms and four legs, and two faces both the same, on a cylindrical neck, and one head, with one face one side and one the other, and four ears, and two lots of privates, and all other parts to match. They walked erect, as we do ourselves, backward or forward, whichever they pleased, but when they broke into a run, they simply stuck their legs straight out and went whirling round and round like a clown turning cartwheels . . . bowling along at a pretty good speed.[2]

These funny round creatures, whirling around backwards and forwards, furnish but a comic backdrop for a fresh telling of the classic tale of the fall of human beings from the grace of the gods. Aristophanes recounts the human offense culminating in the fall: "And such, gentlemen, were their strength and energy [of the globular humans], and such their arrogance, that they ac-

1 Plato, *Rep.* 6.500c.
2 Plato, *Symposium* 189e-190a.

tually tried . . . to scale the heights of heaven and set upon the gods."[1]

The fall is tragic-comic. Zeus does not wish to destroy the human race because the gods enjoy human sacrifices, but he must "put an end to the disturbance" and curb the offensive arrogance of these cheeky round creatures. He decides to weaken each one by half by splitting it in two parts, "as you or I might chop up sorb apples for pickling, or slice an egg with a hair."[2] Apollo helps to accomplish the dirty deed, turning the faces round to the front, so that the sad, torn little half-creatures can walk upright on one set of legs. But the sorry creatures in their new broken form wander about tormented and yearning, mourning the loss of their primeval wholeness.

The punishment sounds comic but rings with a serious truth for its ancient Greek audience: it underscores the crucial importance of humility in human lives and recalls that when humans over-reach their lowly positions in the power chain of existence, tragedy follows swift and hard. Aristophanes' account of Love in the *Symposium*'s debate of that topic ends in uproarious tragedy, as each of the two parts of the once-whole being, lost without its natural mate, goes about "questing and clasping" and clinging desperately to all the wrong partners. The sorry scene rings true for the reader, reminding us what melancholy, pining fools we can make of ourselves when we are in love.

For the Greeks, *hybris* is the greatest evil of the human world because, like earthquakes and tidal waves in the natural realm, *hybris* oversteps the due measure that guarantees harmony and peace. The wrath of the gods will descend without fail upon the arrogant upstart human who gets too big for his mortal britches. Humans must learn to be reasonable, and practice appropriate measure in their desires and their actions.

3. Evil as Unharmonious Competitivism

Plato posits reason and stability in the gods and other heavenly beings and objects alone. In the *Phaedrus* myth of the Feast of Being, human souls falter and fail. The gods are redefined as

---

1 Ibid. 190b.
2 Ibid. 190d-e.

compliant, amenable rulers who keep to their unique domains and parade in harmony.[1] Humans aspire to true knowledge of excellent things but only the "orderly gods" make the steep ascent to the heavens where souls are nourished on beauty, justice, temperance, and "the veritable knowledge of being that veritably is."[2] Humans have the troublesome quality of *phthonos* (greed, egoism, avarice) that causes them to struggle with each other, grasp and claw for their separate interests, and ultimately fall from the heavens to a degraded existence on earth.

The *Phaedrus* myth indicates that the worldview grounded in a love of order cannot help but devalue the things of the world that change and flux and flow. In this view, human beings, with their fickle and steamy passions and their shifting opinions and ideas, and ultimately earthly existence itself, with its troubling unpredictability, comes to be seen as wanting, as more or less degraded and fallen. Mortal existence is a brief "prison" sentence whose fleshy, earthy excesses—disease, ageing, and death—can be overcome by the rejection of the changeable (the bodily, the passions, the appetites) and by rational contemplation of the changeless, in philosophy's "practice of death."[3]

The West believes its values, its systems, and its traditions to be built on the Greek ideal of democracy, where differences are embraced within the common category of "the people" (the demos). But, as we have seen, the love of order, much older and more persistent, favors sameness and uniformity, and only tolerates the people when their troubling differences can be overcome in a common will or a common patriotism that rejects change and supports the status quo. In fact, all major thinkers in the cradle of Western philosophy are suspicious of democracy as the dangerous political system where order is constantly under threat. For the ancients, democracy represents the unpredictable, the irrational, where the dictates of reason are drowned by the cacophony of the uneducated and wayward masses, where evil demagogues toady to the fluctuating desires of ignorants to serve their own wicked designs. The Ancient Greek word for "the many" *(hoi polloi)* is still employed in modernity to voice our

1 Plato, *Phaedrus* 246d ff.
2 Ibid. 247e.
3 Plato *Phaedo* 82d ff.

inherited contempt for the common people of a society. After all, the many cannot be saved from their fickle excesses, because philosophy is impossible for them.[1]

Changeability is the problem. Order is the solution. The love of order recommended to the ancients, and continues to recommend to moderns, the establishment of strong states whose laws (*logoi*) control and stabilize the discomfiting fluctuations in the opinions and passions of commoners. The myth of the "classless society" in the West veils the distinction between commoners and the wealthy and affords the illusion of a common body of folk invested in the state as "We the People."

4. Is Love of Order a Fitting Value for a Democratic World?

Georges Bataille demonstrates, in "Propositions on Fascism" (Bataille, 1985, 197-201), that the ordered state beloved by the West falls on the far end of the spectrum between two extreme possibilities for the structure of states. The model that aspires to perfect order mirrors the timeless realm of the gods, a frozen homogeneous perfection that Bataille names "monocephalic" (from the ancient Greek for single-headed). Like a god, the monocephalic state represents a sacred entity—changeless, eternal, faultless—these values fixed and guaranteed in strict, legal imperatives.

At the other end of the structural spectrum resides the second extreme form of state—the acephalic (without-head) state—disordered, anarchic, and volatile. This state is seen by ordered states as a terrifying heterogeneous "primitive" life-form characterized by "uncivilized" tribal practice, mystical thinking, incommensurable truths, and mad affective experience. Unreasonable. Unpredictable. Mad. People within the acephalic social structure enjoy abundant ritual lives that offer escape from the mundane in orgiastic festivals that involve drunkenness, dancing, blood rites, wanton tortures, self-mutilation and sacrificial murder in the name of dark monster gods. Where the primitive acephalic society is referred to chaos, madness and death, the civilized monocephalic state has overcome all death. Its stable structure boasts a firm foundation where reason, life and prog-

---

1 Plato, *Rep.* 6.493e ff.

ress can be staged.

Bataille's dichotomy of extreme possibilities provides a valuable framework that brings into focus the hidden character of global realities. Without a love for order, societies can collapse into murderous and chaotic tribalisms. But with too much love for order, another dark possibility arises. States can become seen as divine creations, their politics unfaultable, their practices unquestionable, their social traditions infallible, and their laws imperative. Critics of the system are seen as evil outsiders, seeking to undermine the divinely-sanctioned. States must be protected against corruption by these aliens through the legalized violences of police and military.

Intricate, unyielding systems of rules and regulations—passports, licenses, identity cards, forms completed in triplicate, travel restrictions, immigration regulations, police interrogations, surveillance of social and financial transactions among subgroups, "security" checkpoints, departments of "homeland security"—weed out the deviant until criticism has been silenced, threats of rebellion obliterated, and state evolution logically contradictory. Trouble arises in paradise when order is too highly valued. Bataille demonstrates that, as the monocephalic state increasingly closes itself off, it stifles social existence, smothers creative energies, chokes the passion from its citizen-devotees, suffocates their spiritual urges, and reduces all sacrificial activity to mundane utility. When the perfection of the structure is finally accomplished, all life has been squeezed out, all labors co-opted in servitude to the cephalus (head). This culminating stage of development of the state whose greatest love is order, Bataille finally names for the dark reality that it is—fascism.

For Bataille, history moves in endless cycles, and states, being historical entities, can be counted upon to oscillate along the spectrum of structural varieties between the two extremes. Now they come to erection as unitary gods of knowledge and power, which increasingly ossify into rigid totalities with obsessions about order and security; then they explode in hysterical, raging catastrophes, releasing the explosive liberty of life from mundane servitude. The chaotic madness will eventually recompose, drawing itself into a rigid unity, slowly heaving up its stiff divine head, and once again imposing order. Life, set free for a time in chaotic freedom, turns back upon itself, and develops "an aversion to the initial decomposition." History moves continually from the ecstatic bliss of wanton pleasure and the writhing agony of change toward the stasis of safe, reliable, unyielding and ultimately suffocating order, and then back again, in eternal cycles.[1] Time, asserts Bataille, demands both forms in the world—the eternal return of a fixed, intransigent infinitely ordered structure and the explosive, creative, destructive rage of the liberty of life.

We may not readily recognize, in our states, either of the extreme structural forms that Bataille describes—fascist stasis or chaotic ecstasy. Modern Western states, many readers will object, compose a golden mean between Bataille's two economies, aspiring neither to a rigid Apollonian fascism nor to a manic tragic Dionysianism, but to the reasonable *metron* of golden rules. However, it is equally clear that the roots of the Western world are well planted in the fascist drive, in their love of order and changeless eternality. Hesiod and the PreSocratics, as much as Biblical myth, cite a common *arche* of the universe in the good works of a god that renders order from chaos. For the ancients, one head (*cephalus*) is far superior to many; simplicity is beautiful while "the many" compose the detestable *hoi polloi*. The foundational logic that posits order as ontologically and morally superior to messy multiplicity remains an unquestioned assumption embedded in the Western lifeworld, recommending a single, well-ordered political obelisk, stretching high into the sky— erect, proud, rigid, unyielding—over the broadest democratic playing field frenzied with incongruous voices.

Bataille's corpus, from his meditations on the sexual cruelties of de Sade to his ruminations on the colorful anuses of apes, may seem a theater of cruelties, far removed from our reasonable ideas. But his literary excesses are better understood as crafty moral exercises. Bataille's scandalous writings are meant to disclose the ugly truths which we labor conceptually to conceal from ourselves, the dark underside of the order-loving politics of every polite "civilized" human society. The chaotic and messy

---

1 Bataille, "Reflections on the Executioner and the Victim," 198.

extravagances exposed in his philosophy give us a peek into the monstrous ritual tortures practiced in high-security prisons, the illicit sexual excesses that seep into oval offices, and the "Shock and Awe" bloodbath-spectacles that betray projects of "freedom and democracy" as the imperialistic conquests they most truly are.

Bataille holds that states evolve from the ordered into the chaotic and back again in endless cycles. But I suggest, rather, that those ordered societies that attribute their stability to forces of civilization are better understood as faithful to the millennia-long-standing tradition of ritual sacrifice murders whereby archaic human societies rejected difference and carved out a sense of solidarity and identity. On the other hand, those so-called "primitive societies" that were the object of imperial "civilizing" projects of civilization were, in many respects, more civilized, more *humanly* evolved, than the invading conquerors. History does not simply move forward in cycles but every historical stage suppresses an internal paradox. On the dark underside of order, bound up with reason's projects and triumphs, lurks a theater of cruelty and murder, just beneath the polite veneer of "civilized" culture. Just out of the light of productivity and progress, people are torn by conflicting drives: their love of order and timeless security is driven by dark, subterranean forces they suppress and deny.

The violence that floods the globe in modernity claims everywhere to be serving reasonable projects, such as democratizing communists, "developing" other people's lands, promoting industry and productivity, and peacefully intervening between troublesome warring forces. Stable, rigid countries, like England and the United States, roam the globe on the argument of spreading freedom and democracy to primitive, conflicted peoples. But their projects may simply conceal an ugly truth toward which Bataille points: the excessive overflow of chthonic urges. Human beings crave mystical, passionate, frenzied escape from the rigorous rationality of their ordered societies, with the xenophobic monitoring at borders, the constant red and orange terrorism alerts, the rigid socio-economic arrangements, and the numbing mediocrity of their lives in consumer society. The more the state hardens and raises its powerful head in ordered majesty, the more we may expect the inner demons to beckon them from their dreary bleakness to revel in evil's orgiastic festival. Life's erotic drives will out and fulfill themselves in the deathly destructiveness of war and the wanton joy of heroic self-expenditure.

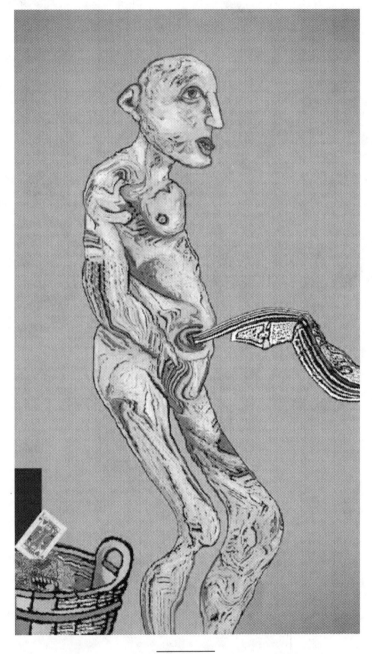

CHAPTER THREE. EVIL IN PHYSIS

Many of us like to dream about retiring from our city lives to the friendly forest or mountain clime, feeding off the berries, nuts and other fruits of a benevolent Mother Nature's bounty, housing ourselves beneath her sheltering foliage and drinking from her sparkling waters. But is nature really that kindly mother, bent on accommodating human needs? Or is nature, rather, morally bankrupt, indifferent to human needs and unsympathetic to our suffering? That most creatures live in justified fear and ruthless self-assertion is an everyday and mundane reality of the natural realm. This is the backdrop reality that explains why most species feed off the others. It really is a jungle out there. Ten per cent of the thirty million living species on the planet are parasites. George C. Williams, one of the godfathers of evolutionary biology, calls Mother Nature "a wicked old witch."[1]

1. Mother's Evil Aspect

Genes-driven will to survival, tempered by the increasing entropy of age, characterizes the way of being in the realm the ancient Greeks called *physis*. Most systems left to themselves run down over time, deteriorating into increasing disorder and

---

1 George C. Williams, *Adaptation and Natural Selection* (Princeton, N. J.: Princeton University Press, 1966).

dysfunction toward ultimate collapse and expiration. Beings are programmed at the genetic level to strive against these odds for survival. Even in the most will-depleting circumstances, such as the Nazi concentration camps, only very rarely did human captives take the easy way out and throw themselves on the electric fences that would end their suffering.

Entropy and will to survival seem to compose opposing forces. On earth and across our solar system, there appears to be an internal dynamic that mediates between these opposing forces and thereby maintains a certain equilibrium that keeps the whole running in an orderly fashion.

The earliest Greek philosophers recognized the contesting forces of nature and named them *enantia*, a term that suggests more than an abstract notion of internal forces but suggests warring opponents or enemies. This recognition prompted Heraclitus to image the cosmos as a strung bow, and to name Strife the father of all things. "It is necessary to know that war is common and right is strife and that all things happen by strife and necessity," and "they do not apprehend how being at variance it agrees with itself: there is a back-stretched connection as in the bow and the lyre."[1]

The ancient philosophers often used the qualities of things to image the perpetual contests between these warring opposites that maintain the fragile balance of the cosmos; hot and cold, wet and dry, just and unjust work against each other—and together!—to hold existence together. Good and evil too compose a warring set. If good is the orderly operation of the whole, the harmonious cooperation of species, then evil in this duality represents the disruptive, chaotic forces that seek to undermine the harmony. What is disruptive has no survival value, so constitutes the evil in the system. From time to time, the disruptive wins out and natural disasters disturb the delicate equilibrium that maintains life as human beings know it. Richly diverse webs of life, elaborately connected ecosystems bound in interconnected harmony, flourish for a time, often by the most fragile of links. But ultimately the disruptive undermines that harmony and entropy or disaster wins out. What threatens that fragile

1 Heraclitus, Fr. 80, Origen c. *Celsun* VI, 42; Fr. 51, Hippolytus *Ref.* IX, 9, I.

balance of beings and tests their enduring harmony could be called nature's evil.

One of the greatest evils that threatens systems is overcrowding. Order is disrupted by density; disorder promotes aggressiveness. Where species grow overcrowded, they tend to increase in aggression toward their own kind. Crowded cats, rats, and chimps have been known to cannibalize each other. Assault, abuse, murder, child abuse, suicide, infanticide and other forms of extreme aggression rise dramatically in human communities that become too dense. The sheer weight of growing numbers threatens the social balance within and among communities, even where shortage of resources is not at issue.

Ironically, natural selection favors those individuals who show the greatest amount of aggression; the aggressive get the most and the best food and the most desirable (healthy) mates and they are able to pass on their genes more effectively. The life forms we find in existence today are the result of hundreds of millions of years of natural selection for fitness, that is, in many species including our own, greatest aggressiveness. Richard Dawkins is the genetic scientist who champions the existence of the "selfish gene."[1] Dawkins argues that genes are unscrupulous; they will do whatever it takes to promote the continuance of their kind. Cheating, lying, ruthlessness, and cruelty are genetic predispositions that grant advantage to those who can skillfully apply these qualities, improving the profit-loss ratio of their holder. All species are subject to the ruthless interests of genes that encourage unscrupulous behaviors.

Species can increase fitness by being nice to each other, favoring close relatives, and being cooperative within their group. But kindness toward strangers is not a genetic predisposition. From the point of view of the selfish gene, sharing outside the kinship group is wasteful and involves unnecessary risks. Humans and animals tend to be naturally xenophobic. Lyall Watson summarizes the situation:

> Generally speaking, if one organism ever does anything to help another it is bound to be either an accident;

1 Richard Dawkins, *The Selfish Gene* (Oxford: Oxford University Press, 1976).

the result of a manipulative deception; a nepotistic act in favor of a close relative; or one of reciprocity that sooner or later will prove equally profitable to the giver.[1]

One of the very few true human universals is the inclination to classify the world into *us* and *them*. This fact leads anthropologist René Girard to name the most crucial and commonplace of human rites to be the scapegoating mechanism and the murder-sacrifice ritual that rejects the scapegoat from the group.[2] Indeed peaceful societies are hard to find. Those human groups who tended to be originally peaceful and naturally democratic, such as the great majority of pre-colonial African tribal societies, have been slaughtered by the more aggressive or have learned the hard lessons of aggression from their oppressors.[3] We may as well accept the sorry fact that "aggression is a part of our furniture," as Watson phrases our genetic situation.[4] But Watson holds out hope that we may avoid the evils toward which our genes drive us: "we have a choice as to how [that furniture] should be arranged."

2. Aggression in the Human Animal

Since Aristotle defined human being as "the rational animal," popular belief has figured the animal part of humans as their evil aspect. This assumption underlies any worldview that defines humanity as a goal *to be achieved*, rather than a species *that we are*. Socrates takes such a position when he defines justice as the *definitive* human excellence, leaving those of us without perfect justice (which is, by Socrates' own definition, all of us) *definitively* less than human.[5] Lionel Rubinoff takes a similar position in his *Pornography of Power*. Rubinoff warns that human urges toward violence are so deeply embedded in our animal nature that our only hope of escaping their destructive effects is in facing them

---

1 Lyall Watson, *Dark Nature* (New York: HarperPerennial, 1997), 260.
2 René Girard, *Violence and the Sacred*, Patrick Gregory, tr. (Baltimore: Johns Hopkins University Press, 1977).
3 See Wendy C. Hamblet, *Savage Constructions: A Theory of Rebounding Violence in Africa* (Lanham, Md.: Lexington Books, 2008). See also Jared Diamond, *Guns, Germs and Steel* (New York: W. W. Norton, 2005).
4 Watson, *Dark Nature*, 176.
5 Plato, *Republic* 353e.

directly and working through our natural impulses, rather than denying their existence. Rubinoff states:

> The repression of man's demonic nature leads inevitably to a search for substitute forms of gratification not only in fantasies but also in direct experiences, such as nihilism or violence.[1]

Ironically, experts on aggression in humans and animals tend not to endorse the animal-within-us theory of aggression. Konrad Lorenz, a primary pioneer in the field of animal behavior study (comparative ethology), in his seminal book *On Aggression*, affirms primitive instincts in the human animal but attributes unrestrained human aggression to our difference from animals, not our resemblance. For Lorenz, animal species enjoyed vast stretches of evolutionary time to develop, alongside their growing destructive skills, the inhibitors that would hinder them from turning their aggressive weaponry on their own kind. Animals kill for food, but that act is not aggression proper; it is no more aggression-motivated than when humans take a steak from the refrigerator. An animal killing his dinner lacks the physiological signals that ethologists recognize as marks of aggression. The dominant males in animal groups do aggressively challenge each other, but they almost always settle the contest without killing the rival.

From the moment our species learned to control fire, however, their evolutionary situation became unique:

> instinctive behavior mechanisms failed to cope with the new circumstances which culture unavoidably produced even at its very dawn. There is evidence that the first inventors of pebble tools, the African Australopithecines, promptly used their new weapon to kill not only game, but fellow members of their species as well. Peking Man, the Prometheus who learned to preserve fire, used it to roast his brother: beside the first traces of the regular use of fire lie the mutilated and roasted bones of *Sinanthropos pekinensis* himself.[2]

---

1 Lionel Rubinoff, *The Pornography of Power* (New York: Ballantine Books, 1969).
2 Konrad Lorenz, *On Aggression*, Marjorie Kerr Wilson, tr. (New York:

Fyodor Dostoevsky's philosophical aspect, sounded through the character Ivan Karamazov in his novel *The Brothers Karamazov*, describes human beings as "savage, vicious beast[s]", but he definitively rejects the equation of human evil with animal nature, asserting "People talk sometimes of bestial cruelty, but that's a great injustice and insult to the beasts; a beast can never be so cruel as a man, so artistically cruel."[1]

Stanford neurology professor Robert M. Sapolsky, in an article entitled "Pseudokinship and the Real War," draws parallels between the aggressive tendencies of animals and humans and attributes these to the reliance on kinship features in distinguishing between "us and them."[2] Sapolsky states: "When it comes to Us versus Them, it's all about who your relatives are. Kin—cooperate with them, defend them in a tough situation. Unrelated stranger—start growling menacingly."[3] The logic, asserts Sapolsky, is older than human time; it is as old as our animal ancestors. But human beings have learned to perfect it. The human reliance upon cognitive ability to distinguish kin from stranger-foe explains human being's greater propensity for violence.

Biologically, explains Sapolsky, the logic of "help friend and harm enemies" rests upon two evolutionary facts: "First, evolution selects for organisms passing on as many copies of their own genes as possible. Second, the closer a relative it, the more genes you share in common with them."[4] Thus, to help out a close relative is altogether (genetically) self-serving; I am actually helping them to pass on copies of my own genes.

The problem for human beings, continues Sapolsky, is that, unlike the deer mouse, the dog or the stickleback fish, who instinctively know their kin largely by the distinctive, genetically based olfactory signature—their peculiar smell—human beings have lost their instinctive capabilities and have a great deal of trouble figuring out just to whom their "kind" amounts. If you

Harcourt, Brace and World, 1966), p. 239.
1 Fyodor Dostoevsky, *The Brothers Karamazov* (New York: Barnes and Noble Books, 1995), 220.
2 Robert Sapolsky, "Pseudokinship and the Real War," *San Francisco Chronicle*, Sunday, March 2, 2003, D3.
3 Ibid.
4 Ibid.

are a muskrat, blood is thicker than water and your nose tells you who to love and who to hate. But, if you are a human, there are no smells to signal where the family ends and the alien begins, so "Us versus Them" thinking can stretch across the human landscape. Since the moral and the social are mutually embedded in the lifeworld, and since humans have lost touch with the subtler arts of distinguishing friend from foe, what does not belong in the immediate social group is likely to be found not merely objectionably malodorous, but morally wanting.

The genetic/biological wisdom of the body dictates that we help those close to us to pass on their genes. In the absence of olfactory confirmations, humans look upon the stranger and our senses let us down. One way that humans deal with this problem is through processes of "pseudokinship," claims Sapolsky. In the face of the unknown other, we ask ourselves: Is the stranger like me? Does he look like me? Does he act like me? Do we share any common features or mannerisms? Customs? Language? Codes of conduct? "Did we play together when we were kids and our moms were off foraging in the rain forest?"[1]

Humans figure out their relations on the basis of cognitive activity. Every time that these questions about identity and difference meet with a negative response, they are taken as clues to beware of the unknown other. On the other hand, when we find similarities, even on a fairly trivial level, we can form "pseudokinships" with the strangest of bedfellows. This process explains the secret relationships of sorority sisters and lodge brothers, enlisted men, members of the gay community, feminists, historians, philosophers, and African American people in general. From those who share a neighborhood to Fred Flintstone's Royal Order of the Water Buffalos, human beings develop similarities to bind our groups—Yo, Bro! Hey, Comrade! Secret handshakes and salutes.

With the erosion of family loyalties and values under the leveling effects of consumerism, industrialization and urbanization, and with the general phenomena of alienation and competitive isolationism (from inner-city slums to rich suburbia) experienced by abandoned elderly, alienated youth, is it any wonder

---

1 Ibid.

that people seek out pseudokinship groups to assuage the sense of isolation and disconnectedness that plagues the modern industrial world? The irony is that we are often as quick to make friends of strangers as we are to make strangers of family and friends, and yet the phenomenon of "Us versus Them" thinking maintains. The more markers of identity we share with our kin and pseudo-kin, the more opportunities exist for those lacking those markers to come up wanting—morally wanting.

When does it all begin? It probably begins in grade school when we remain silent while our classmate is being browbeaten by the teacher; then in middle school when we would rather lose a friend than risk becoming the next target of the cool kids. What keeps people silent at the violation of others? What makes us laugh at ethnic jokes when we don't even think them funny? It is the desire to belong, the fear of rejection from the pseudokinship group, the fear of showing signs that we do not fit, that we are indeed strangers. But it is also the constant conditioning within our kinship groups, through social rituals of inclusion and exclusion, that convince us some people are indeed "stranger" than others, that "legitimate authority" has the right to illuminate and punish that strangeness.

On the battlefield, soldiers report feeling such a profound sense of responsibility for their fellow soldiers that it is not uncommon to take a bullet to save another.[1] What is it that solidifies the relationship among the fighting young men and women over a few mere weeks of basic training, forging bonds that will measure life as their witness? Night-vision goggles, camouflage gear, snorting, spitting, defecating in the woods side by side— these rituals of pseudokinship are designed to foster a sense of familiarity that builds bonds among brothers-in-arms that mimic kinship bonding.

A wealthy palette of ritual life attends the military art, preparing the warrior to meet with the enemy, as well. David Grossman, a psychology professor at West Point and expert in the psychology of killing ("killology"), tells, in his *On Killing: The Psychological Cost of Learning to Kill in War and Society*, that rituals

---

1 David Grossman, *On Killing: The Psychological Cost of Learning to Kill in War and Society.* (New York: Little, Brown & Co., 1995), p. 13.

as simple as drill help to prepare troops for killing.[1] When the troops are marching and their hearts are racing at 300 beats per minute, the frontal brain is switched off and the back brain takes over command, automatically dictating the body to fulfill the task that is to be completed. The task is what the soldier has been learning in shooting practice, to shoot at human-like objects.

Long before he or she stands over against the human enemy, the soldier has been trained to demonize the figure he or she will have to shoot. It begins with killing rituals like shooting practice with human-like figures as targets and endless hours of video games where enemy combatants become less like humans and more like ducks in a shooting gallery of a town fair. Then the ritual of nicknames helps to maintain the fiction of fellow soldiers as family or childhood friends. Similarly, the "human" reality of the enemy combatant can be eclipsed by dehumanizing names—gook, Kraut, slit-eye and the like. Inhibitions increase as the soldier grows close enough to the enemy to recognize the symmetry of their positions. Dropping bombs from on high is easy; shooting at distances not difficult; killing at close range becomes much tougher, but it helps if the face is foreign. In the Second World War, 44% of the American soldiers declared themselves able to kill a Japanese, while only 6% said that of Germans.

During wartime, every society develops rituals of demonization to reconstruct the social imaginary of the populace and make the people more comfortable with the killing that will ensue. The intelligentsia becomes complicit in the ritual manipulations. During the Second World War, American medical journals carried many articles explaining how the physiology of the Japanese differed radically from American folks. The Japanese were almost like another species of being, they reported. Did it really matter if we killed them? Sapolsky names this process "pseudospeciation."[2]

Healthy-minded people do not readily experience complete strangers as a threat to them. In times of social crisis, however, when people already feel threatened, they may look out upon

1 Ibid.
2 Robert Sapolsky, "Pseudokinship," D3.

the world for a scapegoat enemy upon whom to focus their fear. If the differentiating processes that Sapolsky discusses prepare us to make friends where there are strangers, then no doubt crises and a sense of powerlessness and vulnerability prepare us to make enemies of those who do not match the kinship criteria. If these criteria mark out the belonging from the non-belonging, then, since the social and the moral are mutually embedded in the lifeworld, these criteria (and the manipulative forces in the environing communities of belonging that design and publicize these criteria) also mark out the friend/family from the foe/intruder. They mark out the good from the evil.

3. Aggressive Nature Nurtured

Humans are a species of ritual. Deposits at grave sites dating back long before humans acquired the physiological equipment for speech show that, very early in human time, the naked ape had already developed an elaborate palette of ritual around life's crucial paradoxes and crises—death, birth, coming-of-age, marriage, illness, fertility and famine. A ritual event composes a series of performative procedures which bear significance far beyond the acts themselves. Ritual performances are, by definition, subject to the strictest regulation over the time, place and manner of their repetition, and over those granted the authority to perform those acts.

The oldest, the most pervasive, and the most time-honored social ritual, practiced over millennia in the early history of the human species, is the murder sacrifice ritual. Much and worthy research has been devoted to understanding the early forms of that rite of social exclusion and mapping their benefits to the societies in which they served. It is now accepted as anthropological fact that the first human communities came into being by redirecting the aggressions of the group upon an alien passer-by or neighboring group, or upon a deviant within the group.[1] In times of social upheaval, a deviant or alien was located, abused and insulted, chased about in a mounting frenzy, and ultimately murdered (or metaphorically "murdered" through exile from the

---

1 See Wendy C. Hamblet, *The Sacred Monstrous* (Lanham, MD: Lexington Books, 2004), Chapter Four.

community or through torture or beatings that brought on the "death" of unconsciousness). Experts differ on the question of whether human victims preceded animal victims or came later to replace them.[1] But one fact is certain: human communities practiced murder sacrifice rituals over millennia and continued their practice long after that ritual maintained any meaningful resonance with the belief systems or customs of the society.

We may believe that the modern world takes very carelessly any of its lingering social rituals. Polite niceties of social grace—the "After you" at the doorway—seem to fall into disuse when it is convenient. In particular, I speculate that few people would be tempted to accept my suggestion that murder sacrifice rituals continue to hold place in the modern world. However, that is precisely what I shall argue in this work—that sacrifice rituals continue to hold sway over the most profound levels of our identity work. Though today we may believe the god to be dead and ritual (and their later elaborations in myth) to be swept aside by the onslaught of modernity, in actual fact social ritual still reigns over the terrain of individual identity and divides the sacred from the profane. The inside and the outside of the various sites where identity work is carried out are constantly negotiated and renegotiated through social rituals of inclusion and exclusion that define the belonging and the nature of their commonality, and delineate the non-belonging and the manner of their deviance from the group. Alien intruders who threaten to contaminate the sacred spaces of our lives continue to be expelled—metaphorically or really murdered—to purify our sites of belonging. Social rituals continue to establish borders between self and other, sacred borders that give rise to outrage when violated or penetrated.

The more totalizing and oppressive the system, the more fully and rigorously the ritual institutions that hold the system in place embraces social and political life. Violent expulsion rituals have over time become deeply and insidiously embedded in the

---

1 Walter Burkert believes that the Paleolithic hunt ceremony staged the advent of human community as human had to learn to work co-operatively in order to succeed at the hunt of large carnivores. Greek myths like *The Agamemnon* suggest that human sacrifices may have been customary for such purposes as appeasing the gods to guarantee success in war.

social, economic, and political institutions of every social group in every nation, here more sublimated, there more overt, but always at least latently driving people toward violent solutions to the contradictions of their lives. The more that a group has been the target of violence and has suffered in the recent past, the more threatened the group may feel by environing alien presences, and thus the more likelihood exists that, under conditions of social upheaval, they become obsessive, pathological, and violent. Violence rebounds in further violences. Thus victim populations have a great propensity for acting out their past sufferings upon strangers perceived as threatening.

4. Nietzsche on Natural Vitality and the Evils of Weakness

Friedrich Nietzsche has a great appreciation for the Dionysian amoral quality of natural life; "life *must* continually and inevitably be in the wrong [according to Christian morality], because life *is* something essentially amoral."[1] Life flourishes as a self-affirming strength that overflows its boundaries, breaking free from rules and laws and the pessimisms and hyper-moralities of weak and sickened societies.

Does this mean then, for Nietzsche, that natural strength and vitality always fulfill themselves in cruelty and dominatio against weaker beings? Nothing so simplistic is at work in Nietzsche's philosophy. Born of life's overflowing strength and vitality are a plethora of adaptive virtues—forgiveness, liberality, generosity, compassion, and many others. After all, generosity is only a possibility where there exists strength and robust health to support it. Nietzsche confirms that only the robust, the most noble, can afford the great virtues such as forgiveness.[2] Strength translates into an appreciation for others' fine qualities, rather than a petty jealousy of others' assets. Thus the strong are able to celebrate even their enemies, appreciating their winning qualities and taking advantage of their superior endurance and power as opportunities to test and publicly display their metal.

On the other hand, Nietzsche insists that strength permits

1 Friedrich Nietzsche, *The Birth of Tragedy*, Walter Kaufmann, trans. (New York: Vintage Books, 1967), 23.
2 F. Nietzsche, *On the Genealogy of Morals*, Walter Kaufmann, trans. (New York: Vintage Books, 1989), Second Essay, 57-97.

another aspect of noble bearing to display itself: true strength does not take advantage of weakness to raise itself up. The strong refuse to take advantage of the weak, even when the weak are contemptuous and hostile toward them. The strong respond to attack from lesser men with the question: *What are my parasites to me?* The contempt of resentful and petty people can be easily brushed aside when one knows one's own worth.[1] What matters is not what lesser men think, but what I think of myself and what my worthy peers have to say.

The strong do not *react* to petty spitefulness; they do not even see evil in others. This is because the strong person is an *active* self, actively *self*-crafted, honed to a stout robustness and a rigid durability, and polished to a glossy elegance. Their integrity is not jeopardized by the ill will and petty actions of others. The strong can afford the fullest generosity—forgiving and forgetting affronts—because they employ a reckoning system that is noble and gracious beyond trivial-mindedness, malice, and vengeance. According to Nietzsche, the strong live lives according to "a formula of extreme affirmation born of abundance and plenitude, an affirmation without reserve, of suffering itself, of guilt itself, of everything questionable and strange in existence."[2]

The strong are to be distinguished from *reactive*, weak people. The latter are more fragile in their relations with the world, more vulnerable to attack and thus more guarded in their posture toward others. Theirs is a "degenerate instinct which turns against life with subterranean revengefulness."[3] Those riddled with *ressentiment* operate on the strictest reckoning system of reciprocal relations—tit for tat—keeping rigorous accounts of every assault they suffer and plotting with great care every petty revenge.

Nietzsche insists that the thirst for revenge on the part of the weak stems from their dissatisfaction with themselves, more than their dissatisfaction with others. He states:

> For one thing is needful; that a human being should *attain* satisfaction with himself, whether it be by means

1 Ibid. 72.
2 F. Nietzsche, *Ecce Homo*, Walter Kaufmann, trans. (New York: Vintage Books, 1989), 2-3.
3 Ibid.

of this or that poetry and art; only then is a human being at all tolerable to behold. Whoever is dissatisfied with himself is continually ready for revenge, and we others will be his victims, if only by having to endure his ugly sight. For the sight of what is ugly makes one bad and gloomy.[1]

Nietzsche's description of the differing responses to injury practiced by the strong and the weak offers a compelling point of entry to the problematic of evil in nature. It is not so much that the Mother is a wicked witch, as that she is too vital, too dynamic, too Dionysian, to make distinctions between good and evil. Nature is not good or evil; nature simply is. Mother Nature lies altogether outside the jurisdiction of our moral compasses. Nietzsche compels us to admit that, contrary to many people's deepest intuitions, evil is nothing *in itself*, but constitutes a construction in the eye of the weak and resentful beholder. Those who see great evil in the actions and the being of others tend to be *reactive* people, laboring under feeble self-esteem and suffering from life-denying *ressentiment*.

However, this is not to say that because people are weak and resentful, they choose to identify others as evil. It is not so much that people freely *judge* things and persons to be evil or good, but rather, things and persons *come* to us—one might even say "disclose themselves" to the subjective gaze—as always already possessing moral significance. What concerns us in our search for an understanding of evil is the source and nature of the logical schemata that serve up phenomena *as good or evil*. Nietzsche suggests that conditions of life fit us with darkened spectacles through which phenomenal events arise as morally acceptable or morally wanting. What "conditions of beholding" govern that phenomenal event?

Our consideration of Mother Nature as a "wicked old witch" here was launched from the famed metaphor of Williams, godfather of evolutionary biology. And we have seen that his dark view of nature resonates with the phenomenological experience of evil as something that lurks "out there" as a willful force pointedly seeking our destruction. Lyall Watson too posits nature as

1 Ibid.

bent upon human annihilation, or at least heartlessly indifferent to human needs. I suspect, however, that evolutionary biologists have the problem the wrong way around in rendering nature an enemy to human beings. Human beings, throughout human time and most certainly since the dawn of the modern era, have been bent upon reconstructing nature to suit only human needs. As industry lays waste the earth's crust from desert to rainforest, pollutes the atmosphere and the vast water systems, and renders extinct animal and plant species at a rate estimated 1,000 to 10,000 times faster than the natural rate of extinction, humans are the declared enemy of nature.[1] We are clearly gaining the upper hand in the final battle that Ray Woodridge names the "Next World War."[2]

Configuring nature as an enemy to human life casts the battle for survival in the dangerous "us versus them" mode that is counterproductive to the survival of humans or any earthly creatures, and tends to convert environmentalism into a kind of religious, or at least political, movement that must then vie with other religions or parties for people's allegiance. Crucial to the survival of human and nonhuman life on earth is the recognition that the enemy that faces us in the third millennium of the Common Era is not nature, but the erosion of ecosystem functionality. Nature may be supremely indifferent to human interests, but it is not seeking our destruction either. Ecological decline is the enemy, a foe so formidable that it threatens all human and non-human life, all ambitions and projects. Defining ecological decline as the enemy dissolves the battle-line in the "us versus them" logic and places all nature and human interests on the same side of the strategizing table, working cooperatively to solve a problem that threatens everybody and everything's prospects.

---

1 See DK *Encyclopedia of Endangered Wildlife*, CD ROM, produced under the patronage of UNESCO and in consultation with the National Museum of Natural History (Paris).
2 Ray Woodbridge, *The Next World War: Tribes, Cities, Nations, and Ecological Decline* (Toronto: University of Toronto Press, 2004).

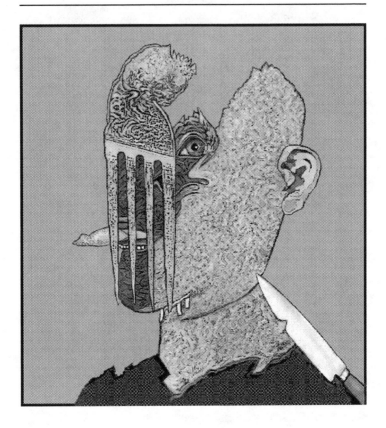

CHAPTER FOUR. EVIL AS SOUL FRAGMENTED AND DISEMBOWELED

Poet and philosopher of the ancient world admit that there is little incentive in the marketplace and the political or legal arena to induce just action.[1] Plato places in the mouth of the tyrannical Thrasymachus an account of popular justice that will later be revealed as the logic of the cave where honors, popularity, and material realities reign and eclipse the concerns of justice. Thrasymachus accurately expresses the non-philosophical view when he frankly admits:

> All with one accord reiterate that soberness and righteousness are fair and honourable, to be sure, but unpleasant and laborious, while licentiousness and injustice are pleasant and easy to win and are only in opinion and by convention disgraceful. They say that

1 In ancient times, sages (*sophoi*) such as Solon had been revered because, in their wise words and in the lived deeds of their lives, they exemplified the hopes and ideals widely shared in the community. By the time of Socrates, the new *sophoi* were more of sophists, doing quite the opposite, trying to tear down the accepted beliefs and values, seeming to tear down the old truths and replace them with nothing but man himself as the measure of all things. The new amoral climate served to underscore a pessimism that was already thematized throughout ancient lore and voiced by Thrasymachus in the first book of Plato's *Republic*: just action is absurd in the real world. See M. I. Finley. *The Ancient Greeks* (New York: Viking Press, 1953), 117.

injustice pays better than justice...the gods themselves
assign to many good men misfortunes and an evil life,
but to their opposites a contrary lot.[1]

General consensus holds justice dangerous and useless: *injustice pays better than justice*. Philosophers rightly feel themselves
out of place (*atopos*) with the world, since their values are loftier
than the pragmatic concerns of the marketplace and law court;
they seek the good rather than the goods of the world.

Since the birth of their art, philosophers have employed the
notion of soul (*psyche*) as the metaphorical image around which
to construct theories justifying the philosophical life over the
non-philosophical life. They employ the image of soul to explore
ultimate questions: What is the nature of human being? What is
the human status in the cosmos? What are people's responsibilities with regard to other human beings and the diverse creatures
with whom they share the planet? Soul provides a convenient
image for fleshing out the relationship between the material and
fleshy concerns of bodies and the immaterial concerns of mind
and morals. Soul helps the ancients to position ethical concerns
about appropriate comportment in a world which offered little
material and concrete incentive toward just action.

Philosophers of the ancient world design fanciful explica-
tions of the genesis of the cosmos, nightmarish accounts of the
fall of humankind from favor with the gods, and utopian visions
of transcendental reward to orient the ethical compasses of human beings as they carve out their treacherous paths through
the "fevered" and "swollen" cities of the world.[2] The PreSocratics
tend to examine the world in terms of the divine breath or fundamental substance that activates matter and causes the myriad
things of the cosmos to arise, and though each early cosmology
is undeniably ethical in its orientation, not until Socrates is the
task of the philosopher explicitly defined as an ethical one.

Plato stages Socrates in the marketplace practicing his philosophical art with any who will listen. The youth of Athens follow as he reduces to absurdity the certainties of the city leaders,
politicians, poets, and sophists. There exists an explicitly ethical

---

1 Plato, *Republic* 364ab.
2 Ibid. 372e.

dimension to Socrates' dialogical explorations: he believes that claims of certainty are the mark of the tyrant, and only humility can render people tolerant of others, good companions and neighbors, and happy individuals.[1] The image of soul figures prominently in each of Socrates' ethical arguments. When he argues the case for the benefit of his art to individuals and the city (in the *Apology*), when he argues for human immortality (in the *Phaedo*), and when he argues for the value of justice in itself and in human lives, Socrates employs the image of soul.

Plato depicts the great master, speculating upon the origin of the soul, its structure, its truest nature, and its ethical calling. The view that he presents of soul, across the Platonic corpus, shifts broadly from dialogue to dialogue. The breadth of diversity in the various sketches has been the cause of much scholarly perplexity. The ancients highly valued simplicity over diversity and complexity; if one account depicts the soul accurately, "Why the embarrassment of riches?" scholars wonder. Most Plato scholars have assumed that the shift expresses Plato's objective rather than Socratic influence. In presenting a smorgasbord of accounts of the soul, scholars assert, Plato seeks to ensure, from all interpretive angles, that human immortality is secured. The variety of explanations of the nature and place of human soul, the argument runs, evidences Plato struggling against *all* odds for the continuation, in one form or another, of the beloved Socrates. Plato's focus on the soul is, by this account, tragic and nostalgic.

Modern thinkers have largely abandoned the notion of soul, arguing that it is an outdated relic of a religious worldview that needs to be tossed in favor of more modern images for exploring human motivations. Modern explorations of human motivations for the acts people distinguish as normal or abnormal, good or evil, tend to reduce human mental and moral life to bodily impulses and chemical reactions in the brain. Certainly there exist good reasons for scholarly abandonment of the image; the notion of soul suggests the traditional philosophical splits— two aspects of existence (bodily and mental) and two realms of existence (earthly and heavenly)—that degrade the bodily/

---

1 Plato, *Theaetetus* 210c.

earthly over against reason and the supermundane. Though I fully acknowledge the problems attached to the notion of soul, I argue in this chapter that ethically-productive babies born of the soul image have been thrown out with the bathwater of the two-dimensions/two-worlds theories. To demonstrate the ethical losses entailed in the abandonment of the image of soul, I explore the rich ethical uses to which that image has been put, using the example of Plato's corpus. Then I demonstrate that a crucial ethical dimension of human existence disappears from philosophical view, as the image of soul grows fragmented in later Plato, and ultimately becomes disemboweled in modernity.

1. Plato on Psyche

Much of what Plato has Socrates say with regard to the soul is spoken in the midst of concerns about death. This has given rise to the conviction among traditional Plato scholars that it is the immortality of the human soul which is the driving force behind many of Plato's discussions of *psyche*. Following the execution of the beloved old philosopher, arguments for the immortality of the soul compose the philosophical means whereby Plato can keep Socrates alive. Yet, in the *Apology*, Socrates states very clearly his philosophical position with regard to death: he does not care in the least whether the soul is immortal or not.[1] Whether death be a great long sleep so sound as to permit not a dream, or a golden opportunity to practice discourse with the heroes of bygone days, Socrates goes happily toward his death. Socrates says to his accusers: "You are mistaken, my friend, if you think that a man who is worth anything ought to spend his time weighing up the prospects of life and death."[2]

Nevertheless Plato goes to great lengths throughout the *Apology*, the *Phaedo*, the *Republic*, and again later in the *Phaedrus* to do this very thing: to weigh up the prospects of life and death and prove death has no claim over soul. If we consider Plato serious in his attempts to prove the immortality of the soul, then a great many difficulties immediately arise, not the least of which is the fact that the proofs are blatantly invalid: equivocation, modal

---

1 Plato, *Apology*, 40c ff.
2 Ibid. 285b.

fallacy, ontological mismatch, and special pleading are but a few of the many faults of these arguments. Moreover, only one valid proof is ample to secure life after death, so does Plato offer so many variants to clinch the deal?

Generally accepted among scholars is the fact that Plato explores the philosophical landscape well beyond the merely skeptical horizons that Socrates had originally charted. Plato never contradicts his master in the important questions he explores; on the question of death and the nature of soul he seems to agree with Socrates that whether the soul is immortal or not is not the important philosophical question. The crucial question, for Plato as for Socrates, is the ethical question: how to live rightly here and now. Socrates states in the *Apology*: "I suggest, gentlemen, that the difficulty is not so much to escape death; the real difficulty is to escape from doing wrong, which is far more fleet of foot.[1]

Plato employs the image of soul to stake out a moral claim in the human being. Plato radically overturns previous philosophical understandings of the human soul in the interest of his ethical mission. His arguments for immortality throughout the *Apology*, the *Phaedo*, the *Republic*, and the *Phaedrus* review PreSocratic and popular notions of soul, expose their moral and ontological weaknesses, and then recraft the concept *psyche* according to a new moral imperative. Just as in the *Gorgias*, Plato redefines *techne* to include professional ethics, in his arguments for immortality of soul, he redefines *psyche* to include a sense of moral calling.

In the cosmological arguments of the *Phaedo* (The 'Cyclical Argument' at 69e6-72a1 and the 'Causality Argument' at 102a10-107b10), Plato relies heavily on Anaximander's and Heraclitus' view of the cosmos as the battlefield of *enantia*, contraries that are martial enemies unto death. In myth, ultimate moral norms keep the balance between these warring powers; in philosophy, it is the *arche* (*pneuma, apeiron* or *logos*) that keeps the cosmos from falling into chaos. Since each of these arguments views the soul as mere breath of life, together they voice how the soul was understood before Plato's time. This view, consonant with

---

1 Ibid. 39a5-a7.

the cosmology of Anaximenes, reasserts the old mythological imagery which portrays departed souls as the wailing shadows of Hades whose existence is non-functional, insubstantial, and non-cognitive.

The cosmological arguments prove greatly disappointing to the prospect of immortality. Within the context of the cosmos, only the impersonal breath of life continues, an impersonal life-force shared with every housefly. Plato employs the oblique method of intentionally fallacious argumentation to demonstrate that the human soul in its cosmological context grants only the *fact* of continued life and not the *quality* of life. To win immortality at the cosmic level is to win one's individual extinction. Where singularity is undervalued, everybody loses.

The second and third proofs (the Argument from Recollection at 72e3-78b3 and the Argument from Kinship or Affinity at 78b4-84b8), remedy the problem of a too general immortality by claiming special status for the human soul based on its unique relationship with the world of Forms, perfect ideas of excellent things, such as justice, and courage, and the Good. These proofs demonstrate that soul is naturally destined to rule over the bodily since it is more akin to the Forms than to the visible, corporeal world of mortal things. The soul, like the objects of its rational gaze, is immortal and ontologically special.[1]

The soul's specialness grants more than singularity; its special relation to excellent things demands that it reflect and practice those excellences in its daily affairs. Plato's equation of knowledge with virtue demands that soul's cognitive functioning equates with moral functioning. Life becomes richly human and its continuance meaningful. Furthermore, now that Plato has shown human soul to have a specifically cognitive/moral aspect, he can begin to speak of specificity of identity: Socrates' soul *is* Socrates. The new coinage points away from the fundamental sameness of all humans, and toward the unique moral quality of each individual.

The proofs for immortality that Plato offers in the *Phaedo*

---

1 T.M.Robinson notes the ambiguous status of the soul as described in these arguments. On the one hand, the soul is denied kinship with the world of sense, but on the other hand, it is clearly alien to the Forms in fundamental ways. (*Plato's Psychology*. Chapter 2.)

draw extensively on earlier views of *psyche* but what is really novel and indeed revolutionary about them is that, together, a wholly new human being comes to view. Heraclitus' and Anaximander's world soul was sentient, cognitive, and very much alive but it was a general cosmological principle, which assigned no special status, no moral imperative, to human souls. Heraclitus and Empedocles both acknowledged a moral aspect in the human character but, when referring to this, they abandoned *psyche* and shifted to the term *daimon*. Anaxagoras held *nous* to be a general cognitive principle which ordered the cosmos, but gave it with no moral underpinnings, and human soul had no special moral task.

Plato gathers together this rich heritage of thought about *psyche* but invests it with that specifically moral/cognitive dimension which reorients the meaning of human being in the direction of an ethical ideal. The new definition of *psyche* proposes human beings as naturally, definitively just. Soul, by virtue of its kinship with the forms, gains simplicity and distinctiveness and independence. Plato sets soul apart from the rest of the natural world by assigning it a special ontological status that raises the ethical compass of the human well above the worldly horizon.[1] The message in this shift of definition is clear: the realities of the cave may reflect the state of worldly existence, but the soul is destined for nobler ends than wealth or power or glory; it is meant to aspire to higher values, to practice virtue, and reflect excellence in its daily affairs. Human soul, like the individual form, though whole and distinctive and independent, is nonfunctional and useless and its existence meaningless except in so far as it practices excellence.

The stark choice for the individual is exposed in this new definition of the soul: either one aspires to excellence and reflects virtue in everything one does, or one relinquishes one's

---

1 In the *Laws* at 803b, Plato acknowledges the ambiguous ontological status of the human soul when he states having in them only a small portion of reality. In a bitter and lengthy tirade, the body is adamantly devalued as the prison bars through which we see the world. The soul is clearly distinct from the body and it can no longer be defined merely in terms of what it is but is to be determined in terms of that to which it aspires. Quite literally, you become what you behold.

humanity, falling not merely to the level of the naive and amoral creatures of the earth, but to the execrable rank of the many-headed beast (*Republic* 588-589). Excellence, if difficult, becomes accessible, through a rigorous program of cognitive practice—philosophy. Since the cognitive/moral condition of the human soul is determined entirely by its objects of cognition, concrete measures can be undertaken to attune the soul to the good. By choosing carefully one's bedfellows in the cave, by attending exclusively to edifying thoughts, and by cultivating habits that are good and just, one's soul can be reshaped in accordance with its divine inner reality and the forms. The importance of the philosophical art, with its constant practice of self-examination, is underlined by this definition of the soul. The consequences of the non-philosophical life of moral lassitude are equally exposed: to become caught up in the race for the goods of the cave (wealth, glory, power) is not merely a cognitive loss. The plummet into moral forgetfulness is both a moral loss and an ontological loss—the collapse of one's humanity!

Plato expounds upon the moral aspect he has granted to soul when he offers yet another proof for immortality at *Republic* (608d3-611a2). This argument also introduces an explicit definition of evil as internal degradation of the soul. Unrighteousness, intemperance, cowardice, and ignorance may not kill the soul—indeed the evil man can outlive the good and just man—but the soul cannot be destroyed from within by these evils.

This image too portrays soul as detachable from body, and again confirms soul as naturally just and good. Evil appears as unnatural, inhuman, and linked with bodily distractions. What this argument adds to Plato's previous accounts of soul is a heightened sense of moral urgency. What we *gaze* upon in the cave, what we *eat*, where we *walk*, and with whom we *speak* and interact involve concrete moral ramifications for the being we will *be*. Plato is affirming the old adage of his master: a man can do far more harm to himself than ever another can do him harm.[1]

---

1 This is consonant with Socrates' assertion in the *Apology* (30c-d):" Neither Meletus nor Anytus can do me any harm at all; they would not have the power, because I do not believe that the law of God permits a better man to be harmed by a worse." Again, at 41cd, Socrates states: "Fix your minds on this one belief, which is certain- that nothing can harm a good man either in life or after death."

The only true evil that can befall a person are those of her own deliberate choosing and these can be avoided by rational deliberation. Sound judgments grow easier with the cognitive/moral practice of philosophy.

In Book IV of this dialogue Plato offers the image of the tripartite soul, an image that recurs in the *Phaedrus*.[1] Here Plato shows that the taint of the body remains with the soul even between its earthly lives when the soul is no longer its prisoner. The deep association of the bodily with the rational in this new view of the souls provides Plato the opportunity to consider more fully the complexity of human nature.[2] The idea of the body serves as a metaphor for the immediate realities of the world; the soul's inability to break free of the taint of the body, even in its physical dissociation from it, shows that, despite soul's special ontological status, soul's natural place is earthly. This suggests the deeply relational character of the soul, its profound interdependence with the things of the world. The being of other beings is inscribed within the soul, as it were.[3] The body is the vehicle through which soul finds itself at home on the earth, the medium through which its life is lived. Soul may enjoy kinship with

1 Traditional Plato scholars generally agree with W. K. C. Guthrie that the soul, for Plato, is essentially simple and only appears composite because of its association with the body. Hackworth (*Phaedrus* p.76) sees this as an unresolved contradiction in Plato's own mind to the end. W. K. C. Guthrie (*Plato's Views on the Nature of the Soul*) and E.R. Dodds (*Plato and the Irrational Soul*) refer to the passions and appetites, admitted here as parts of the tripartite nature of the soul, as the mortal parts of the soul to be abandoned as it achieves perfection. F. M. Cornford refers to the three parts as manifestations of a single fund of energy, Eros, directed through divergent channels toward various ends (*The Doctrine of Eros, the Unwritten Philosophy*. Cambridge: Cambridge University Press, 1950. 71.) F. Coppleston takes the opposite view of the doctrine of the tripartite soul, stating that we can hardly be justified in supposing that Plato ever abandoned it. (*A History of Philosophy*. New York: Doubleday. 1944. 208.)

2 This is described as the ectoplasm theory by T. M. Robinson, *Psychology of Plato*. Chapter 2.

3 Edmund Husserl makes a similar discovery phenomenologically, when he sets out, in the Fifth of his *Cartesian Meditations*, to reduce the ego to its most egoistic state (Section 45), to banish all otherness from the realm of consciousness. Far from the charges of his critics, that phenomenology entails a radical solipsism which threatens its viability as philosophy, utter isolation of the ego from the things of the world, including other egos, turns out to be an utter impossibility.

merely rational objects, but the flesh is how living becomes real and authentic. But body is also the medium of moral fragility. It is the umbilical cord through which the "Great Beast" of unreflective tradition conveys its dangerous truths into our souls. [1] To posit the duality of body and soul is a literary sleight of hand, which permits Plato to expose the dangers of an unthinking acceptance of historical and cultural truths posing as eternally valid.

Plato makes use of the imagery of soul when it suits his ethical purposes, but he will readily alter this imagery to suit the ethical problem at hand. Later in this same work (*Republic*), Plato returns to a view of the soul as simple and non-composite (611a ff):

> It is not easy...for a thing to be immortal that is composed of many elements not put together in the best way, as now appeared... to be the case with the soul... But to know its nature we must view it not marred by communion with the body and other miseries as we now contemplate it, but consider adequately in the light of reason what it is when it is purified and then you will find it to be a far more beautiful thing.

That Plato is not wedded to a single view of soul but alters the image to suit his ethical purposes is best depicted in the *Phaedrus* where at one moment the soul assumes the tripartite structure, and at yet another, soul is singular and unique. Plato also introduces in this dialogue yet another new image of soul as the principle of movement in the cosmos. In this depiction (245c6-246a1), the soul's immortality is no longer dependent upon its simplicity. Soul is the self-moving, source and beginning of all motion. [2] All-Soul (*Psyche-Pantos*) acts universally to tend and move body, as the benevolent caretaker of inert and helpless matter. Its immortality is presented as a function of its definitively kinetic nature: if movers cease, the whole universe would collapse. [3]

---

1 Plato, *Republic* 493.
2 This claim is repeated at Laws at 896a1-b3.
3 Plato joins Orphic *psyche* and Ionian *physis* in this new understanding of the soul, Plato's first attempt to deal with *kinesis* (motion, change)

This view of the soul does not guarantee personal immortality any more than the cosmological arguments of the *Phaedo*, but it does expand the moral functions of the soul.[1] Moral life becomes trickier than mere suppression of desires and passions, or careful maneuvering through worldly cave-cities. Now fulfillment of the soul's moral destiny will be tied up with other beings, in an ethics of care and responsibility; solicitude, attention, and guardianship of the helpless and the needy will be demanded, tough tasks that begin with the ordering and harmonizing of one's own multiple elements.

Evil, previously explained as the failure of recollection of virtues through preoccupation with the base and unedifying, now emerges as a lack of self-attunement, a disharmony among the various aspects of the whole soul. Evil becomes more than mere psychological self-conflict; it is a shirking of one's duty toward others who are more needy and helpless than oneself.

Does Plato really believe in the immortality of the human soul? This cannot be maintained with any degree of certainty.[2] It seems more likely that the question of what comes after death is not nearly so important for Plato as the questions concerning *how* to live more justly in this life and *why* one might choose to

---

as an element in the cosmos. (J. B. Skemp, *The Theory of Motion in Plato's Later Dialogues*, Cambridge University Press, 1942). Skemp explains Plato's need to accommodate the idea of motion or change within his definition of the soul: "What has been achieved is simply the recognition that the Forms do not explain the dialectician who studies them and that therefore some more comprehensive metaphysic is needed to embrace them both."

1 This is further developed in the myth at the end of the work (247c ff.). Here the soul is described as a charioteer and two winged horses, one white and of noble character and the other black and of base character. The nobler horse is said to represent the passions and the baser the physical appetites. The difference between the gods and the fallen soul of man is now located in the character of their respective horses. The horses of the gods are both of noble lineage, so the god is able to drive his chariot, whereas the human carriage is pulled this way and that by the unruly steeds. The *phthonos* which has no place among the divine host, however, is assigned to the human soul as a whole, and not simply to the steeds. This suggests a certain nature, one of envy, competitiveness, and greed, which is not localized merely in the appetites or the passions but infects and affects the entire human being and diminishes the individual's ability to virtuously interact with his fellow.

2 C. Ritter, *The Essence of Plato's Philosophy* (London: Allen & Unwin, 1933), 282.

---

pursue such a goal in a world where justice is a disadvantage. Plato, like many philosophers of old, employs the image of the soul because it is a valuable metaphorical tool which can be richly textured with ethical meaning. His various accounts of the nature of the soul expose what evils stalk human life, but they also offer concrete suggestions on how to accomplish the inner harmony and the communal integrity which constitute justice.

2. The Fragmentation of Psyche in Plato's *Republic*

Plato's dual depictions of the soul in the *Republic* offer an opportunity for meditation upon the complex internal and external forces—some unequivocally evil, some potentially good—against which the soul must struggle. The *Republic* offers a third view of the soul that is generally overlooked in studies of Plato's psychology: the soul *writ large* is the metaphor under which two cities are constructed in words (the first, Socrates' favored "simple city" and the second "city in *logos*"). Plato scholars have tended to ignore the simple city and to name the second city Plato's "ideal" state. The Greek text does not support this reading, however. It is crucial to an accurate reading of the *Republic* that we acknowledge that Plato presents the second state as a city *in idea* (*eidos*), not an *ideal* city in a moral sense.

From Book II to the close of Book VII, the two cities are fashioned, the first abandoned when the young Glaucon and Adimantus insist that an ideal city must include luxuries that Socrates omits in his simple city. Book XIII analyses how internal evils befall the state and undermine its integrity, and Book IX closes with an explicit re-statement of the purpose of the construction, affirming the uselessness of the political blueprint for the establishment of just states and its value as a model for the *writ small* image of the individual soul under which purpose the state was constructed.

Socrates' simple city is Plato's *writ large* image of the healthy soul, and the second city in *logos* represents the *writ large* image of a soul "fevered" and "swollen" due to an uncontrolled desire for luxuries.[1] The simple city demonstrates the workings of justice as harmonious and peaceful community of diverse interests, its

---

1 Plato, *Republic* 2.372e.

parts happily fulfilling the tasks most suited them without encroachment upon the rightful prerogative of other neighboring interests. The simple city demonstrates that human beings are complex and that many aspects of human existence must be juggled to maintain the integrity and happiness of the whole person. Plato's ethical message is explicit: the task of internal management is simpler if desires are kept within reasonable limits.

Next Plato passes the image of soul *writ small* through a strange and frightening lens that issues in a state that Socrates admits from the outset is "fevered" and "swollen." This enlargement, the second city in *logos*, represents the soul inflamed and engorged from an unwise unleashing of overblown desires for the things valued in human cities—honors, power, and wealth. The second city brings into relief how the human soul comes to be dehumanized in the city, how people can become splintered into less-than-human fragments when luxuries are allowed to hold sway. The city in logos that Socrates, Glaucon, and Adimantus construct through the ten books of the *Republic* are valuable for their painstaking consideration of how human life comes to be leveled—from the ideal of integrated human flourishing to the base self-conflicted, inflamed ideals of the fevered marketplace.

At the close of the construction of the ideal city in Book IX of the *Republic*, Plato has Socrates state explicitly that it matters not at all that this political structure cannot be found on earth, or that it will likely never come into being. The *Republic* is not constructed with the aim of delineating the truth of any actual state, nor to provide a blueprint for any political entity. That was never the intention of the construction. The purpose of the construction is explicitly stated at the opening of Book II (358b) in Glaucon's challenge to Socrates:

> what I desire is to hear what each of them [justice and injustice] is and what potency and effect each has in and of itself dwelling in the soul but to dismiss their rewards and consequences [in the world].

Justice is shown in itself in the simple city; justice and injustice are demonstrated in the second city. Socrates re-affirms at the close of Book IX that the purpose of the constructions was not to fashion an ideal state but to demonstrate the opportunities for justice and injustice in *individual* souls. The city in *logos*, Socrates affirms, is "a pattern . . . for him who wishes to contemplate it and so beholding to constitute himself its citizen."[1]

This thought experiment in political construction is undertaken with the express goal of displaying the human soul *writ large* that we might see with greater clarity the dynamics of the inner functioning of the individual soul. By following the patterns of interaction among the soul's diverse parts, we may witness the spiritual climate which best favors the cultivation of justice. Simple is best, Socrates shows, sketching an idyllic country life of simple satisfactions, but the young boys complain that human beings want more than the simplicity of pigs; human living, they argue, demands luxuries (2.372d).

On the long hot night of a festival, when the promised feast was not tabled, the proposed horse-races not attended, the intended prayers not offered, the spectacular entertainments forgone, Socrates constructs two cities in *logos*. The greatest spectacle of the evening occurs in the house of Cephalus, as the rich old munitions-factory owner shuffles off to perform the sacrifices that seal his business with the gods, and the young boys, spellbound, draw near to the sorcerer-philosopher who conjures in a carnival mirror two images of the soul—healthy and unhealthy.[2] Funhouse mirrors distort and twist as they enlarge. Simple images may fare well with little distortion. But overblown grotesque images grow more exaggerated still, frightening, ominous. While moments of true likeness can flash across their surfaces, funhouse mirrors reflect terrifying images in their mercurial facades. The *Republic*'s swollen reflection, the city in *logos*, is just such an aberration. Its truths are twisted, its beauty deformed. Thus, the image of the city in *logos*, considered as a political treatise is ludicrous, deceiving, and terrifying.

The *Republic*'s mirror will reproduce the unhealthy soul, greatly enlarging its dimensions. The image which rules in that

---

1 Plato. *Republic* IX.592b.
2 The discussion of justice and its intrinsic value in human life arises in response to Thrasymachus' definition of justice as the advantage of the stronger and to his claim that the tyrant is the happiest of men. Thrasymachus reasons thus:...you must look at the matter, my simpleminded Socrates, in this way, that the just man always comes out at a disadvantage in his relations with the unjust. (*Republic* I.343d)

mirror is that of the philosopher-king. He is the kindly shepherd of the state, tending and protecting the welfare of its ward components and promoting the general sense of harmony which is the social and political bond of the citizenry. Under the philosopher-king's benevolent care, the state happily prospers. The music gently plays to soothe the soul of the guardian shepherd-dog, the gymnastic games order and tone their beautiful bodies, and the citizenry in general goes about its most natural business with the contentment and satisfaction of well-fed sheep. This idyllic scene of everyday life in the city in *logos* could be pictured set in the sun-drenched meadows of the philosopher's perfect world, far beyond the entrance to the cave, well removed from the ugly battles and compromises of the real world.

Yet the reader remains unconvinced. The tone, the style of discourse, the setting in the sultry port-town during the festival of the underworld goddess, and above all the frantic sense of urgency which fires this discussion and carries it through the remainder of the ten books of this monumental work disrupt the serenity of that happy scene, and undermine the hope that true justice could ever be achieved in the state at large or in the individual soul.[1] The utopian nature of the city in *logos* is not what troubles the reader most. As we follow the details of its construction, we become haunted by the sense that the *Republic*

---

1 See *Republic* 1.327a, 1.354a. The dialogue is set in the port town of the Piraeus during the festival of the dark goddess, Bendis. Bendis is one of the underworld goddesses to whom the witches in MacBeth refer. She is one of the forms of Hecate, imported from Thrace, home of the mother goddess. She is connected with Artemis (huntress, hostile to humans, especially males) and has associations with Dionysus. Plato's choice of this time and place for the *Republic's* setting suggests that dark and hostile forces of the underworld rule this discourse. For literature on the setting of this dialogue, see W. K. C. Guthrie. *A History of Greek Philosophy.* Vol. IV. (Cambridge University Press. 1975, 434-449.) and Martha C. Nussbaum. *The Fragility of Goodness.* (Cambridge University Press. 1986, 136-139) and John Sallis. *Being and Logos.* Indiana University Press. Bloomington. 1996, 312-320). On style of discourse, Socrates, in this dialogue, barely feigns his usual style of good-natured dialectical inquiry and outright orates much of the construction of the ideal city. By this, Plato is suggesting that the truths about important matters like justice had better not be left to mere chance occurrence. This is further demonstrated by his underlining of the importance of well-intended belief in that dialogue. That belief comes to be justified even if it requires a noble lie to hold it in place. (*Republic* 3.414b. c.f. 3.389b ff., 5.459c ff., and *Laws* 2.663d ff.)

is something of a grotesque caricature of a city. Socrates admits from the outset that it is fevered and swollen, but proceeds in any case.

The result is a state that is anything but a portrait of human flourishing. It offends our intuitive sense of justice. The reader had expected, following the exposure of the limitations of a non-reflective ethic demonstrated by Cephalus, that the ideal city would nurture a self-reflective ethic whereby the Good might come to be chosen as the best option in a thoughtful life.[1] Instead, moral education is instilled through the sub-conscious by gymnastics, carefully selected nursery tales and music; the body, rather than moral reasoning, will become the instrument for education. In any case, the mass of the people will be excluded wholesale from the benefits of education, and well they might wish to be. The educational process is an experiential and intellectual straitjacket. It is purgative, restrictive and radically intrusive.

Life in this distorted polis reduces the human being from the psychologically complex site of singularity (that soul is in the *Phaedrus*, for example) to a single narrow task: that of the good citizen. Indeed in this constricted world, the human being *becomes* his function in the state, his education addressed merely to that end, his entire life, both public and private, defined by his civic responsibility. Individual happiness is forgotten, in the complete subordination of the individual to the state. Difficult to fathom is the idea that the state can be said to be happy, when its parts are not individually so. The life of the guardians most clearly exposes the problem with this utilitarian logic. For the best human being, the state exercises a ruthless control over every detail of life: family values disappear along with the breakdown of the family unit as we know it. Wives and children are shared, love-making reduced to eugenics. Children who do not know their parents are raised by the state so that all distractions from their education can be eliminated. A rigorous purging in art

---

1 Cephalus is a genteel and cultured old gentleman who represents the ancient ways of authority and tradition. But his candid report of the worldly and otherworldly benefits that can be purchased by his wealth and political success betrays the flaws in an uncritical and non-reflective ethic.

and literature intrudes even into the nursery. The only music to be heard will be melodies chosen by the state. Communal property. Communal sexual partners. Communal homes and meals.

As a politics, this state is humanly unacceptable. The beauty and the truth of the soul's just workings are lost in the distended image which emerges from the *Republic*'s mirror in Socrates' second sketch. When the Whole Soul has been fragmented into the many citizens of the state, when self-control has become dominion by a powerful elitist group with secret knowledge, imposing their *raisons d'état*, when lies have become noble, and the political strategies deceit and manipulation, we no longer have a blueprint for a state that fosters full and happy individual lives but a sure recipe for the totalizing closure which breeds tyranny and fascism. With the reflection from the one simple city to the "fevered" and "swollen" fullness of the luxury-ridden state, a single self-disciplined soul is shattered into disparate citizens who are *classed* according to their functions in the polis, controlled by a web of lies, and ruled by a king whose good will we must trust, because his function and methods look dangerously like those of a tyrant. The funhouse mirror distends an image of a world grotesque, fragmented, and dehumanized.

The tradition of Platonic scholarship has been mistaken in reading the city in *logos* as a city that is ideal, a model for justice in states. Plato is explicit about his intention in the *Republic*'s constructions. Plato demonstrates justice in the individual soul through the image of the healthy simple city; he demonstrates both justice and injustice in the individual soul when he presents the "fevered" and "swollen" second city of the *Republic*. If we look upon the city in its political aspect, we see the injustice of fragmented human lives. However, when the scene shifts back to the soul *writ small*, the possibilities for justice come into view anew.

The distortions of justice in the constructed state are a function of the mirror in which Plato performs his reflections. This is, after all, a funhouse mirror, fashioned on a carnival night for the amusement and the edification of the foolish boys who believe that luxuries are the stuff of human living. This mirror, as it enlarges the workings of human communities and their challenges to justice, renders an impossible state: "the city whose home is in the ideal . . . I think that it can be found nowhere on earth," laments Glaucon (9.592ab). Does it matter whether the fevered image can be rendered real or not? Plato has Socrates deny this explicitly when he tells Glaucon:

> perhaps there is a pattern of it laid up in heaven for him who wishes to contemplate it and so beholding to constitute himself its citizen. . . . it makes no difference whether it exists now or ever will come into being. The politics of this city only will be his and of none other.

Glaucon then confirms: "*That* seems probable." Justice enters the realm of the possible, and indeed the probable, when we consider the *Republic*'s construction, not as a pattern for politics, but as a regulative ideal for a singular life.[1] When people pattern themselves after its ideal design, what was grotesque and indeed inhuman gains not only viability, but also regains its just aspect. Plato has told us that the truth of things is seen only in the light of the good (*Republic* 6.508a ff.), so consider what good is accomplished when the soul adopts the model of the city in *logos*.[2]

When the individual lives by the second city's austere pattern of guardian education, she cares little for private property, gladly sharing things in common with friends. She puts the good of the community first, treating others as brothers and sisters, treating all children as one's own.[3] She is wise, like the philosopher-king, but not intellectualizing. Rather, she expresses her knowledge of justice in just action, no matter how ridiculous or strange she may appear to others around her. Through her constant and rigorous practices of bodily health, her nurturance of harmony through gentle music and edifying tales, she comes to

---

1 Plato, *Republic* XIII demonstrates that such a politics soon breaks down under the weight of reality.

2 Thus Plato, *Meno* 81de, 86b. Here Socrates dismisses the Sophists' dilemma as contentious argument that makes us lazy, music in the ears of weaklings. c.f. *Phaedo* 91b. We see what true inquiry is, when we see what good the best inquiry does us.

3 Hannah Arendt recognizes this important truth in Plato's Republic. She states: It is a common error to interpret Plato as though he wanted to abolish the family and the household; he wanted, on the contrary, to extend this type of life until one family embraced every citizen. See Arendt, *The Human Condition*. (Chicago: University of Chicago Press, 1958), 223. See also Plato, *Statesman* 259.

embody a gentility and a public-spiritedness so entirely spontaneous and natural that she is unaware of these qualities in herself. She nurtures in herself a passionate and courageous spirit, a
temperate appetite, and a wise intellect, letting each of these elements flourish without one element running amok, destroying
the harmony of the whole, and causing needless grief to herself
and others. In wisdom and justice, she lets her humanity flower
and she becomes a comfort and inspiration to others. Above all,
she loves justice with a passion and practices it in everything she
thinks and does, knowing intimately its nobility, the beauty of
its truth. She despises injustice, cries out against it wherever she
finds it, and battles it with all her courage.

3. Modernity's Self: Humanity Disemboweled

As the modern age dawned, humans began to recognize in
the imagery of the soul a childlike dependence on otherworldly
powers. As their scientific prowess grew, moderns explored the
secrets of the universe and challenged the hegemony of nature
over human destiny. Creators of a universe of technological mir-
acles, humans entered a new phase of wanton *hybris*. Dismissing
the gods from their service, human beings took upon themselves
their fate. Henceforth the inquiry into the good life would comprise speculation upon the possibilities to which rational human
beings might aspire, unfettered by the inconvenience of ethical
considerations. The image of the soul failed to serve adequately
the new heroic function. Burdened as it is with metaphysical
and religious overtones, it favors only bad conscience for the free
and spontaneous individual.

In the godless dazzling of the twentieth century, in the ethical desert of today's consumer world, the image of the soul is no
longer congruous with the new understanding of human flourishing. A new image is deployed, one better suited to the climate
of democracy's sanctification of individualism and freedom, one
which reflects the new ethic of self-actualization against a limitless horizon of possibilities. Now that the *death of God* has been
proclaimed, individuals need answer only to the inner call of
personal dreams and goals, rejecting as antiquated and *unnatu-
rally* self-limiting the moral codes of cultural and historical tra-

dition. The inherently moral notion of psyche is replaced with a self in mere self-relation. The individual, divinized in his radical singularity, assumes his freedom in full.[1]

This age we consider an unqualified success: micro-medicine, genetic engineering, rational exploitation of the riches of the environment, leaping advances in military technology. We can travel the circumference of the earth in hours, send messages around the globe in nanoseconds, conceive babies in test tubes, and generate energies of cosmic proportion on the head of a pin. Yet we cannot feed the hungry, shelter the homeless, or soothe the myriad ills of the forgotten masses of the globe. We cannot get along with our neighbors, or close the swelling gap between the empire of plenty and the underworld of desperate need.

Martin Heidegger, long before the moral shockwave of the Holocaust rocked the certainty of his philosophical world, voiced his concerns for the directions being taken by modernity. His urgent warnings gain greater poignancy considered against the backdrop of the Nazi sympathies that he would come to share for a time and then never live down.

> This Europe, in its ruinous blindness forever on the point of cutting its own throat, lies today between the two pincers, squeezed between Russia on one side and America on the other... the same dreary technological frenzy, the same unrestricted organization of the average man [characterize each]. At a time when the farthermost corner of the globe has been conquered by technology and opened to economic exploitation; when any incident whatsoever, regardless of where or when it occurs, can be communicated to the rest of the world at any desired speed; when the assassination of a king in France and a symphony concert in Tokyo can be experienced simultaneously; when time has ceased to be anything other than velocity, instantaneousness, and simultaneity, and time as history has vanished from the lives of all peoples; when a boxer is regarded as the nation's greatest man, when mass meetings attended by

---

1 See also Plato, *Republic* 573c: "the madman, the deranged man, attempts and expects to rule over not only men but gods."

millions are looked on as a triumph—then, yes then, through all this turmoil a question still haunts us like a specter: What for?—Whither?—And what then?[1]

Where indeed do we go from here? Heidegger's student and confidante Hannah Arendt made the focus of her life's work the effort to understand how mistaken loyalties (such as Heidegger's allegiance with the Nazis) take shape, how a person's mind can become so pervasively colonized by the twisted myths of propaganda that fascism can begin to look like a salvation. Her words are more relevant now than when they were first written. Hers is a post-Holocaust philosophy whose insights into the problems of modernity are crucial at the dawn of the new millennium. She directs our attention back to the values that Plato proposed as edifying for our souls, and demonstrates the poverty of modern life in comparison with the *vita activa* of the ancients.

Arendt does not pretend to capture the truth, regarding either modernity or history. She is not concerned with an exact account of how life was lived in the ancient *polis* or how it ought to be lived now. Her broad generalizations about an ideal time in the "life of the mind" are not presented as an accurate historical account of how life in fifth century Athens was lived but is meant to suggest an alternative way of conceiving human life.[2] She does not pretend to describe modern reality but offers a gross oversimplification of life in modernity, whose exaggerations are meant to be functional and practical, as they allow her to juxtapose idyllic visions of the ancient good life with nightmarish portraits of Western life at the dawn of the third millennium.

Arendt offers in her *The Human Condition* a compelling account of modernity's sickness.[3] She explains the erosion of human identity as a function of the alienation of humans from their most natural condition. Humans, by nature, are beings whose destiny is to inhabit the earth. The full human life lives out its earthly destiny when it offers rich opportunities to fulfill the

1 Martin Heidegger, *An Introduction to Metaphysics*. Ralph Mannheim, tr. (New Haven: Yale University Press, 1959), 37-38.
2 John McGowan, *Hannah Arendt*. (Minneapolis: University of Minnesota Press, 1998), 35.
3 Hannah Arendt. *The Human Condition*. University of Chicago Press. Chicago. 1958.

various aspects of a complex identity, imaged in Arendt as the realms of labor, work, and action. Arendt echoes Plato's complex treatment of the human soul in the *Republic* when she calls upon modern Westerners to fulfill the natural destiny of our species by enjoying a multifaceted life, with opportunities to exercise the passionate, appetitive, and rational aspects of ourselves.

The good life needs the happiness of labor as it wraps the household in the security of a common truth and a singular goal: attendance to the demands of corporeality and its consequent deferral of death's eternal threat. But it also requires opportunities for work. Work, for Arendt, is the activity of creative exercise, distinct from the merely futile labors that grant continuance. Arendt sees the world of work as a realm of mysterious privacy where the individual regenerates the self, sheltered from the mortal fate, as well as revitalizing the species through the production of human artifacts that outlive their individual creators. In labor, the mortal imparts to his finite life a measure of permanence and durability that it could never otherwise attain. Through the worldliness of work, human beings extend themselves in time beyond the limits of the single lifespan.[1]

Through her fascinating account of the *vita activa* in ancient times, Arendt demonstrates how human life has degenerated in modernity, under the sway of capitalism's voracious ethos of material consumption. Seeking material gratifications alone, modern human beings have become enslaved to the realm of the merely futile. In the ancient polis, the good life began only where the endless cycle of bodily needs was satisfied and the grip of the eternal enslavement to mere life broken.[2] The realm of the private household, where *animal laborans* and *homo faber* labor and work, exist in order to support the public life, where one can distinguish oneself by pursuits and demonstrations of excellence.

The ancient polis was the arena of speech and action where uniqueness and excellence (*arete*) blossomed forth and went on public display. Only public acknowledgement of greatness ensured its reification. Action and speech in the political sphere

---

1 Arendt writes:...this world itself is meant to outlast and transcend them all. *Human Condition*. p.7.
2 See also Aristotle, *Nichomachean Ethics*. i.5., 1096 a5; *Eudemian Ethics* 1215a 35ff.; *Politics* 1337 b5.

confound the futility of mortal life. In the founding and preserving of political structures emerges the condition for communal remembrance of the exploits an individual human life. In speech and action, individual greatness is etched into the analogues of a history of human civilization.

Action and speech, for Arendt, comprise the only dimensions of human life where people are directly related, not buffered from the next by things or matter. Thus, action and speech comprise the crucial conditions of human plurality.[1] On the worldly stage of plurality, humans unfold their humanity, blossoming into interactive and relational beings, where together they fulfill their earth-bounded destiny. While all aspects of the human condition have their political dimensions, the human community lived in action and speech is the *conditio per quam* of all political life.[2] It rests in the fact of one man's being like his human neighbor, yet utterly unlike any other single example of his kind. Arendt states, "Plurality is the condition of human action because we are all the same, that is, human, in such a way that nobody is ever the same as anyone else who ever lived, lives, or will live."[3]

Arendt's account of the *vita activa* echoes Plato's tripartite image of the soul, and develops Plato's tripartite life as modeled in the *Republic*'s blueprint. For Arendt, the human condition can only be fully filled where biological and productive desires have been satisfied and there are opportunities in the individual life for development and demonstration of one's unique excellence. The diverse aspects of human being, fragmented in modernity by a fevered and swollen materialism, can be bound together again in the whole human life, if one follows Arendt's model for the human condition.

Arendt echoes Plato in another respect as well. She insists that the modern failure to achieve the human condition of the *vita activa* that fulfills our humanity means more than a loss of individual happiness; it means a global collapse of the human task.

---

1 Plato, *Phaedrus* 246ab.
2 It is not at all clear that Arendt means political in the modern definition of the term. Her usage has little to do with rule of a state and more to do with personal freedom of interaction. For a wider interpretation of this term; See Fred Dallmayr, *The Other Heidegger*. (Ithaca: Cornell University Press, 1993), 50-51.
3 Ibid. 8.

The collapse is so broad, claims Arendt, because humans are be-ings who do not merely exist for ourselves or for our moment in time. We exist always toward a future. The three dimensions of the human condition, for Arendt, are bound together and pro-pelled in the direction of eternity in the pursuit of a common ob-ligation that stretches beyond itself: the obligation of preparing and preserving a world for future generations. We must always also use our present to prepare for the constant influx of new-comers, strangers who must be provided for. The ethical task Ar-endt assigns to human beings is undeniable and irrevocable. The task expands the meaning of human life, granting it a greatness that exceeds the sum of the activities performed for the sake of nutrition, reproduction, distinction among peers, and historical repute. The *vita activa* fully lived is much greater than the indi-vidual generally appreciates: human beings are called to expend their present in the interest of a future of which they can never partake.

We have seen that in Plato, the soul is always already ethi-cally implicated in its world and called to a self-limitation for the sake of harmonious community. The rich image of soul dif-fers radically from the mere self seeking self-fulfillment, typical of the modern era. Arendt shows that humankind in the modern era has become alienated from the natural, earthly, and inter-connected dimensions of its existence. She suggests a complex of unfortunate factors to explain the leveling of the *vita activa*: the disappearance of the public arena of human activity, the de-generation of human life from the pursuit of excellence to the meaningless ideals of consumerism, and the common confusion of wants with needs.

The ideal of human flourishing has degraded into the greedy and covetous pursuit of mere survival and material accumula-tion. The degradation of human ideals parallels the deformation and fragmentation of the soul into the disconnected and dis-jointed shard of a free and spontaneous self.[1] Human being as a

---

1 Plato posits *phthonos* (greed, avarice, covetousness, competitiveness) as the quality which separates the human soul from the gods in *Phaedrus* myth; it is the cause of the quarrelling and the breaking of wings which destines the fall of the soul from the parade of the gods on route to the Feast of Being. (247a)

site of the realization of the *vita activa* is no more. Human existence now is driven by the yearning to deny human earthliness,
depart from the bowels of the planet, and establish ourselves as
universal beings, whose domain is the whole of outer space. But,
in pursuing this desire, claims Arendt, we have set ourselves ex-
istentially adrift, alienated from the earth mother, and homeless
in a universe where neither earth nor sun are orienting centers,
nor welcoming abodes for the human species.

How did we come to this? Modernity is under the incontest-
able hegemony of the scientist, answers Arendt. The utilitarian
logic of scientific discovery—knowledge for its own sake—un-
derpins all human creation. Plato showed the effects of materialism on the soul through swelling and distortion. Arendt shows
the effects of the scientific mania for measuring and graphing,
by showing how our world has been shrunken and distorted.
People now consider their earthly home coldly from a distance
out in space.

> For whatever we do today in physics—whether we
> release energy processes that ordinarily go on only in
> the sun, or attempt to initiate in a test tube the pro-
> cesses of cosmic evolution, or penetrate with the help of
> telescopes the cosmic space to a limit of two or even six
> billion light years, or build machines for the production
> and control of energies unknown in the household of
> earthly nature, or attain speeds in atomic accelerators
> which approach the speed of light, or produce elements
> not to be found in nature, or disperse radioactive par-
> ticles, created by us through the use of cosmic radiation,
> on the earth—we always handle nature from a point in
> the universe outside the earth.[1]

The centerless worldview of modernity, Arendt claims,
leaves us fragmented from each other and disemboweled from
the planet.[2] In this view, Descartes is no more the father of the
modern world than is Galileo.[3] Arendt underlines the hybris of
modern science and the risks involved in the supermundane

---

1 Arendt, *Human Condition*, 262.
2 Ibid. 272.
3 Ibid. 271.

powers it now holds.

Science controls much of our lives in ways that can no longer be recognized, understood or challenged. The scientist's secrets are encrypted in a tongue lost to the world, and scientific expertise lies far beyond the critique of those it governs. Worse, the science is not concerned with the ethical implications of its knowledge. Driven by the *hybris* of a limitless horizon of possibilities, the subject of his inquiry is the *how?* and the *what?*, rather than the *why?* of knowledge and human discovery.

Rumors of the depths to which the soul might sink in forgetfulness of its true nature and its divine calling haunt Arendt's writings as they haunt the Platonic corpus. Plato insists on the inner beauty of the soul, when justice is its compass and guardianship its mode of political life. In the *Republic* (611b ff.), the soul's true beauty is said to resemble that of the ugly encrusted sea-god Glaucus, god of prophecy and messenger of Zeus, who aids good men with his just counsel, and soothes them in their dissonance one with another.[1] Plato says of Glaucus:

> [His] first nature can hardly be made out by those who catch glimpses of him, because the original members of his body are broken off and mutilated and crushed and in every way marred by the waves, and other parts have attached themselves to him, accretions of shells and seaweed and rocks, so that he is more like any wild creature than what he was by nature—even such, I say, is our vision of the soul marred by countless evils.

Plato is affirming that the beauty of the soul is redeemable, no matter what its present condition. But, like Arendt, Plato recognizes that redemption of the soul's true beauty will require a radical reorientation of present values. It will require a turning of the soul and the body away from the distorted realities of the modern cave, and away from its twisted ideals.

Arendt too is attempting to redeem the beauty of the human self and the richness of a truly human life, by reinserting the ethical into the modern understanding of happiness, responsibility, and belonging. Arendt offers redemption from the unpredict-

---

1 Jason and his crew of heroes are visited by Glaucus as they quarrel over the disappearance of Herakles.

able, chaotic fate human beings now face, a remedy for the bar-
ren futility and instability of modern life in the twin faculties of
forgiveness and promising. Forgiving can undo the ill that people
do to each other, releasing the future from the curse of the past.
Without forgiveness, the deeds of the past are like "sins hang-
ing like Damocles' sword over every new generation."[1] Binding
oneself through promises serves too can mend the fragmented
modern world by setting up in the ocean of uncertainty, which
future definitively represents, islands of security that grant con-
tinuity and durability in human relationships.[2] The twin arts of
forgiving and promising are the tools essential to the making of
a future more suitable for the arrival of newcomers and strangers. They may serve as well as the existential glue to mend the
fragmented self of the modern era.

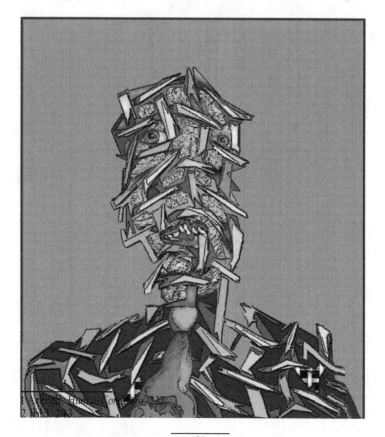

1. *The Human Condition*, 237.
2. Ibid, 243.

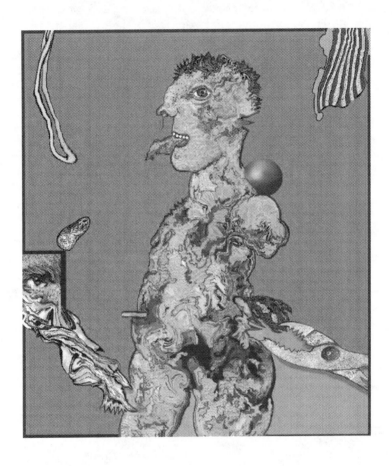

CHAPTER FIVE. INNOCENT EVIL AND THE EGO

In a world of finite space and limited resources, each life must be understood as purchased and maintained at the expense of other lives. We feed off other species. We consume more than our rightful share of the resources that feed life. We exist in the place of some other. Mortal existence is, by definition, murderousness of other possibilities for life. The living subject, caught up in its worldly projects—consuming, enjoying, savoring— lives life alongside others, but also in the place of others who might have been, others perhaps more deserving of life—kinder, gentler, more generous, more peaceful—than I.

Postmodern thinkers, such as Emmanuel Levinas and Hans Jonas, offer this stark phenomenological assessment of mortal existence to jar us from the comfortable thoughtlessness of our Western super-abundant lifestyles. In the wake of the Holocaust, many philosophers have given a new urgency to ethical concerns, attempting to jar complacent consumers of the modern era to a "thinking" posture that presses the free and autonomous Western subject to re-assess the "how" of their wasteful living. Naïve assumptions about the just deserts due the "civilized" peoples of the earth have justified the greed and hedonism of Western peoples that leave third world countries in dire poverty and hopelessness. The notion of history as progress and the prejudice that Western societies epitomize social and intellectual progress have served to render our lion's share of the earth's resources as simple innocent pursuit of happiness, disconnected from the collective fate of the tens of thousands of lives lost daily, expended to support our economic hegemony over the planet.

1. Innocently Egoist and Alone

Mortal being is appropriative by nature; something has to die for me to feed myself, to feed life. Emmanuel Levinas posits consumption as the very mode of mortal existence, the structure of earthly dwelling. Whether I am laboring, lodging, enjoying, knowing, engaging with others, or secluded in my solitary life adventure, I live consumptively amongst others who also live to consume. I persist by feasting upon the bounty of the planet, by indulging and pleasuring in the voluptuous real of the elemental, frolicking in the infinite depths of living beyond the mere sides appropriated in my living.

The elemental ground that sustains life, rich as it truly is, remains necessarily finite, empirically limited in its ability to sustain living beings—hence the daily hunger suffered by one in five children in North America, and the death by hunger and hunger-related diseases of over 30,000 non-Western children around the globe every single day. There is only so much of everything to go around; life for the vast majority of people is lived in the misery of want. It is for this stark fact that Levinas highlights the murderousness of life.

Since consumption is the very mode of mortal existence, life's violences are then inevitable. We can hardly avoid our murderousness, a fact underscored in Levinas' apt phrasing of mortal existence as an "innocent egoism." Levinas states of the mortal condition:

> In enjoyment, I am absolutely for myself. Egoist without reference to the Other, I am alone without solitude, *innocently egoist and alone*. Not against the Others, not "as for me..."—but entirely deaf to the Other, outside of all communication and all refusal to communicate—without ears, like a hungry stomach.[1]

---

1 Levinas, *Totality and Infinity*, 134. (Emphasis mine).

Without "reference to the other," each mortal existent is necessarily—*phenomenologically*—blind to the violences by which existence is purchased each and every day. Life's murderousness does not come into subjective view because those who pay the daily price of my over-consumption languish far from my subjective gaze. Thus subjectivity is lived as innocent—"innocently egoist and alone."

In the essay "the Ego and the Totality" Levinas explains how subjective blindness occurs, but here the subject does not come off so innocent.[1] Violence emerges as a function of self-focused, other-forgetting concern. I fail to see others whom I violate because of an ontological confusion:

> A being that has life in the totality, lives as though it occupied the center of being and were its source, as though it drew everything from the here and now, in which it was nonetheless put or created. For it, the forces that traverse it are already forces assumed; it experiences them as already integrated into its needs and its enjoyment.[2]

The confusion is "ontological" because it constitutes a wrong-headedness about the world and our status within it. Since Copernicus, we have been aware that our planet is not stationed strategically in the center of the universe; the sun does not rise and set for our collective human benefit alone. A human-centered worldview would be easy to bear if the objective of the cosmic drama were the good of the whole human species. But Levinas is not charging the species with a general ontological confusion; he is charging Western individuals with a self-serving hedonism that attends to their own needs and wants and overlooks the vast masses of their human fellows. Levinas calls the subject's mistaken ontological centrality *cynical*, a term that he means in the philosophical sense. The *Cynici* or Cynics were members of a philosophical school founded by Antisthenes (died 336 B.C.E.). Cynics refused to share in the community of their neighbors, they rejected the morals and customs of their fellows, and they chose to live like dogs (*cunos*) in the dirt, in

1 Levinas, *Collected Philosophical Papers*, 25-46.
2 Ibid. 25.

barrels, in the countryside.

The ancient Cynics consciously—thinkingly—chose to live like dogs to make a philosophical point in rejecting polite society and the wealth and honors that held sway in the polis. Levinas' subjects are not thinking dogs, but thoughtlessly doglike; they do not, like the ancient Cynics, reject the false values of their societies, but they live their society's vapid materialism like faithful disciples, unquestioningly, thoughtlessly. Suffocated by self-interest as they make their way in the world, a subject takes up projects of pleasure and of use of other proximate beings, but never really makes a genuine connection with others. Living beings are holed up in their "domiciles," worlds unto themselves. Being's very *esse*, states Levinas, is inter-*esse* (inside-oneself)—self-interested self-investment in one's continuance. The curious self-enclosure of the lifeworld of each and every subject makes for a social setting that is unmistakably Hobbesian:

> Being's interest takes dramatic form in egoisms struggling with one another, each against all, in the multiplicity of allergic egoisms that are at war with one another and are *thus* together. War is the deed or the drama of essence's interest.[1]

Living being composes not simply an innocent adventure of happy enjoyment and useful preoccupation with continuance, but the very acts of living that grant sovereignty, individual identity, corporeal security, and homeliness—the labors of the domicile—frustrate the possibility of "human" engagement, reducing the possibility of community to "allergic egoisms." Communities are, according to this view, an order of jealous warriors confronting each other in common warrior-pose. The essence of *esse* is not merely isolated, lonely, monadic living-alongside-others, but it composes "the extreme synchronism of war."[2]

In their equality of rapaciousness, the most expedient strategy for isolated egos is to submit their warring consumptiveness to reciprocal political arrangements. Mutual limitations may restrict individual sovereignty but will permit a truce in the war of all against all for the purpose of exchange and commerce. So-

1 Levinas, *Otherwise Than Being*, 4. (emphasis mine)
2 Ibid.

cial contracts. Leviathan's rulebook. A rational peace that serves self-interest's interests. But these agreements, however sophisticated, serve only ever inadequately because, tells Levinas, in a free subject's self-interested vision, "every other would be only a limitation that invites war, domination, precaution, and information."[1]

Mortal existence is dark in Levinas' description—murderous, allergic and bellicose. People are like dogs wrestling over too little meal, hunters moving from prey to prey, warriors from war to war, "like a stomach that has no ears" for the wretchedness of others, without the compassion (from *com* and *passus*, meaning feeling or suffering with) that, for many, defines *human* existence. Mortal life seems far from "innocently" lived, if by innocence we mean free from evil consequence to others.[2] This mode of dwelling is inevitable, Levinas suggests; self-interested egoism is simply how life is lived. Is there no way out of the mortal dilemma of "innocent violences?"

2. Subjective Innocence Unveiled

The earliest epic tales recorded in Homer and Hesiod evidence that heroic egoism is deeply embedded in the Western lifeworld. In the grand epic tales and in the tragedies of classical times, the heroic subject opposes himself to the tragic inevitability of his death-bound existence with free, spontaneous, high-handed action that defies the fate that threatens and indeed encompasses his possibilities

Since the Greeks carved out the notion of *aristos* as the "good" exemplified in the aristocratic hero, their peculiar virtuousness could not be disentangled from the manly virtues of *arête*. Nor could that notion of virtuousness be altogether separated from the haughty purity and incorruptibility of the Greek gods to whom the hero stands as half-blood.[3] The virtues of the Greek heroes reside in action—audacious, manly action that calls for the manly qualities of courage, fortitude, audacity, perseverance in the face of hardship, and unquestioning loyalty. Odysseus does

---

1 Ibid., 119
2 In his use of the term "innocence" Levinas means to highlight a phenomenal experience of freedom of guilt and responsibility.
3 "Hero" derives etymologically from *eros*—lover, daemon, half-god.

not wait patiently in his mountain home, praying for the gods to release him from his evil fate; he charges out into the world to defy that fate, faces his destiny at the crossroads, and saves damsels distressed by monsters. He challenges the very gods in their cruel predictions. That is why, whatever the ghastly outcome of heroic action, the heroes remain exemplary, worthy of emulation. They are purified by their tragic futile gallantry, elevated by their tireless spirit half-way to the lofty heights of divinity.

In many ways, their heroisms are moral failures (killing fathers and marrying mothers are judged contemptible by the moral standards of most societies), and yet the agents of these acts remain heroes. No matter if their deeds are moral failings, their exemplariness resides in their intention to do good, an assumption that continues to configure notions of justice in the present day. The ethic of noble heroism, as it has come down to us from the Greeks, posits the blameworthiness of the agent not in the effects of his deeds in the world but in his intention to do evil or good, intentions judged according to reason. The hero has good reasons for action, and the unfortunate fallout of his acts is mere collateral damage.[1] Good intentions purify bad effects in Homer as in Levinas, where the violences of the heroic adventurer are named innocent.

3. Heroic Adventure in Homer's Iliad: A Levinasian Reading

More than anywhere, the manly Greek virtues of arete are displayed upon the battlefield. Homer's *Iliad* pictures generations of noble men fighting alongside their princely brothers for noblest of causes: defending the honor of their fallen damsels, avenging the deaths of their comrades, expressing their righteous indignation at injustices they or others have suffered. So

---

1 It is noteworthy that the Greek heroes do not release themselves of blameworthiness for their effects in the world so readily as do modern Westerners. Western notions of justice rely on the notion of guilt only for intended harms. Odysseus did not intend to bring about the ill fate dictated by the gods, but, when his fate was fulfilled and he had inadvertently killed his father and married his mother despite all his efforts and intentions to the contrary, he cursed himself and levied his own punishments for his deeds. He plucked out his own eyes and sent himself into exile for his misconduct. The gods finished the task with the pollution of divine curses to Odysseus's family that spread over generations.

righteous is the hero's war, always fought for the "right reasons," that even the gods descend from the heavens to fight alongside the heroes on the battlefield. Time and again, the hostilities peak, the tide of the battle rises, challenging a glorious warrior to flee the thrusting sword. Fate rears up in the face of courage and threatens to dash the hero to naught. But heroic pride and relentless spirit drive him on to victory.

The *Iliad* is nothing if not a tale of competing egoisms, fighting to the death to defend their rights and honors. At times, the struggling egoisms turn on each other. Agamemnon, having already sacrificed his daughter to the winds of war, challenges another prince, the great Achilles. Having lost his war-bride prize to prudent negotiation, Agamemnon seizes the beautiful Briseis, prize of the proud Achilles. Agamemnon admits his simple motivation for this injustice when he crows:

> Thus you may learn well
> How much greater I am than you, and another may shrink
> From likening his to my power and contending against me.[1]

Achilles is so humiliated and frustrated by this injustice that he refuses to join the battle, a loss that threatens the victorious outcome of the war. Incensed by the dishonor accorded him by Agamemnon, Achilles retires to the whitening waves of the boundless sea, weeping to his mother, the goddess Thetis. The great hero seems crushed to a whimpering child. But the gods hear his cries and he will not have to wait long for his revenge. The gods guarantee that heroes receive their due rewards. Agamemnon's turn for humiliation comes swift upon the monstrous deed whereby he had dishonored the hero: a very short few days later he must humble himself, weeping and pleading to Achilles to return and turn the tide of battle. Agamemnon, the supreme commander of the avenging forces of Helen, comes to know the bitter taste of humility and the harsh sorrow of pleading in vain.

The *Iliad* records the rise and fall of heroic pride in bloody episodes of glorious vengeance. The ideals we see displayed in this epic remain with us to this day in the Western world, con-

---

1 Homer. *Iliad*, Lines 185-186.

figuring self-understanding and dictating noble action against the wrongs of a decadent world. The *Iliad* is one of the greatest war epics and is generally considered a shameless glorification of the horrors of war, but perhaps there is a deeper message inscribed between the lines that record the rise and fall of the tide of battle.

It is a striking feature of the *Iliad*, and perhaps its most telling mark, that it depicts again and again throughout the grand fray a curious moment of truth that hushes the din of battle and stops short the drama of war. Each hero in turn finds himself, in a singularizing instant, as it were, *lifted* from the fray, in a limbo of sensibility, "face to face" with a demand for mercy from a pleading supplicant. At the height of his glory, each hero experiences this moment, as though fate were extending to him one fleeting chance to show his true human substance. Each hero has this opportunity to break the pattern of overblown pride that dictates brutal vengeance. Each has his chance to respond more compassionately to the trembling alien before him, shrinking under his sword, pleading for mercy. But time and again, the weapon sinks into a disarmed and helpless supplicant, sunk to its knees and pleading. Time and time again, the hero triumphs over a defenseless dying man, describing to him in vivid detail the outrageous disgraces that his body will suffer after his soul has been dispatched. In the "face to face" of the heroic encounter, might is right and the weaker is crushed without mercy.

I am suggesting that, in the final analysis of this great war epic, in the failure of each hero in turn to respond in a more compassionate, more human way to his pleading victim, violence is the sole victor. The glory of Agamemnon over Achilles is short-lived; the glory of Achilles over Hector equally so. The death of Achilles brings but brief joy to the Trojans, the annihilation of Troy empty conquest for the Achaians. Never does it occur to the reigning hero that the supreme test of his power lies not in the thrusting of his deadly sword but comes as the challenge to stay his cruel weapon and spare the life of another. Never does it occur to the hero that snuffing out the life of a defenseless supplicant is an inherently cowardly act.

In my reading, the *Iliad*, that great epic of war, composes a theatricalization of the weakness of heroes, not a display of their virility. Intoxicated by power and bloodlust, heroes ultimately take the path of *least* resistance—driving their weapons into the already defeated, the living dead. That superb indifference that the powerful exercise over the weak is the weakness of the hero, bringing each in turn to the timely deserts of hollow victory and bitter justice.

In the *Iliad*, as in all wars, no one goes home a hero, whatever his heroic acts throughout the glorious phases of the war. Only violence triumphs when the strong crush the weak. And, since violence has a terrible necessity to repeat itself in ever more ingenious and brutal forms, the war does not end when the spoils of battle are divided and the heroes retire to their homelands, but violences continue to rebound in their societies long after the war has ended. The rebounding chapters of warrior violence put in question the reasonableness of wars. But reasonable words fall upon deaf ears in societies that share heroic ideals. If an inferior (as Thersites) pronounces them, he is punished into silence. If a great man pronounces them, he is named a coward and a traitor to his country and to the god.

Levinas is writing in the shadow of one of the grandest (if by "grand" we mean large and overblown) historical moments of heroic adventure. Hitler and the National Socialist movement was, after all, an "ontological adventure" of immense proportion and enormous consequence. Hitler's national and racial hyper-pride was not content to control Germany's borders; he was committed to redesigning the world, imposing a "new world order" that expressed his vision of social justice. Levinas' unfortunate experience with the Nazi *lagers* provides him with insights into the tragically egoistic nature of existents, and helps him to recognize the consistency between Hitler's grand adventure and the imperialist adventures that compose the history of Western civilization. Having survived one diabolical domicile, Levinas is intent upon exposing to modern Western subjects our general proneness to violence, a proneness bound up with the heroic ideals that underpin Western value systems and configure their traditions and institutions. A heroic *ethos* drove the European conquerors across half the globe, slaughtering, pillaging, and enslaving simple tribal peoples. The Holocaust was a singular horror but it had many prologues in the history of the West.

Levinas, having suffered the rigors of war, having lost much of his family to Hitler's heroic vision, having passed many nights in the cruel Nazi prison camp under sadistic guards and cruel *kapos*, recognizes the weakness of this "manly" virility. The greatest power of the *lager* was its ability to reproduce in its victims reflections of its own cruel nature. Survivors tell that the most shocking aspect of the death camps was their ability to quickly reduce the most compassionate human being to "a deaf ear" and "a hungry stomach," interested only in his own survival A prisoner very quickly became a heroic "totality" there—a world unto itself, closed up upon its own needs, shut off from the pleading cries of others, overwhelmed by the exigencies of its own survival, hoarding its crust of bread. "Pure nature," Levinas terms this state. Pure nature "is no one's, indifferent and *inhuman* nature."[1]

In "pure nature," people live dogs' lives, struggling with one another in endless wars over hollow scraps of victory. But can life be given a higher meaning than this? May one choose an existence higher than "pure nature"? Levinas has a proposal—a higher tender than social contracts between struggling and allergic egoisms that simply postpone the war. We find this proposal in the notion of "thinking being" that he opposes to the "innocent violence" of living being that we share in common with dogs. "Thinking being" is another dimension of existence that opens to more "guilty" subjects who carve out a space of passivity in the midst of the dog-eat-dog war of all against all. This does not mean that "thinking being" can put an end to the murderousness of being. It cannot cease the violation of neighbors, nor put a stop to our dogged consumptiveness. "Living being" does not—cannot—leave off its violent ways. Levinas states:

> Is not essence the very impossibility of anything else, of any revolution that would not be a revolving upon oneself?[2]

Self-interest is not a negotiable aspect of living. It composes the very event of living. Violence *is* life. We are, all of us, like "galley slaves" shackled to each other and to life, in a great chain of

---

1 Levinas, Collected Philosophical Papers, 29.
2 Levinas, Otherwise Than Being, 82.

murderousness. The murderousness of life is not a problem that can be solved except in death, when one steps aside *substantially* to make room for another life. Mortal existence is an easy, plea-surable, genuine and simple consumption. We have become so accustomed to its murderousness that we award "military hon-ors and virtues" to the most murderous ones about us.[1]

Moral existence is far from the easy, simple life of the self-pleasuring, other-using subject. It is far from the "path of least resistance" pursued by the hero's sword. Perhaps that is why it is also so seldom accomplished. As Spinoza tells in the closing words of the *Ethics*: *"all excellent things are as difficult as they are rare."*[2] Rare, but not impossible. Similarly, Levinas leaves the tiniest loophole in the necessary murderousness of life. In this loophole opens the possibility that essence can live other than interested, "otherwise than essence." Levinas challenges us to seize that possibility when he states:

> The happiness of enjoyment is stronger than every disquietude, but disquietude *can* trouble it; here lies the gap between the animal and the human.[3]

Violence may be preventable after all, if a subject can but attend to the disquietude—live in awareness, and be-come a "thinking being"—"thinking" about its ways of engag-ing with others, and letting that thinking inform its modes of being-in-the-world.[4]

To seasoned scholars of Levinas, this claim will be jarring to the ear. After all, Levinas states repeatedly throughout his corpus that violence is the very mode of mortal existence and that good-ness cannot be *actively* pursued. The Good is not something that can be realized through willed and purposeful action; it cannot be cultivated by design. Levinas repeatedly insists: Goodness, like the god, can only "pass by" when the good is torn from the agent—in "possession," in "obsession," against every intention and energy of will.

This explains why Levinas alters ever so subtly his moral

---

1 Metaphors taken from Levinas *Otherwise Than Being*, 185.
2 Spinoza, *Ethics*, Part V, Prop. XLII, n.1
3 Levinas Totality and Infinity, 149.
4 Hannah Arendt, *The Life of the Mind*, IV. 197-216.

discourse in altering his metaphors between *Totality and Infinity* and *Otherwise Than Being*. The generous "host" of *Totality and Infinity* is replaced by the "hostage" of *Otherwise Than Being* that finds itself without recourse, without freedom to act or to refuse to act, without the resources to fight or to flee. The host, Levinas recognizes, is not passive enough for the passivity of "undergoing" that is required of the most ethically challenging moments in human life. The good stands outside the hedonistic domicile, and "befalls" the unsuspecting subject, tearing the hero from his adventures.

4. The Just War Waged Against War: Blueprint for an Active Ethos

I contend that Levinas lays the groundwork for an *ethos* of *active* goodness. I find a blueprint of this *ethos* encoded in the concept of the "thinking being" that Levinas opposes to mere "living being" in the essay, "The Ego and the Totality." And I find it in the closing words of his final masterpiece, *Otherwise Than Being or Beyond Essence*:

> For the little humanity that adorns the earth, a relaxation of essence to the second degree is needed in the just war waged against war, to tremble or shudder at every instant because of this very justice. This weakness is needed. This virility without cowardice is needed for the little cruelty our hands repudiate.[1]

"For the little humanity that adorns the earth," Levinas repeats. One of the most important moral lessons that Holocaust survivors like Levinas gleaned from their cruel experiences in the Nazi *lagers* was that *human* life is not about the power to triumph over others. Any and every sorry soul, when the going gets tough enough, will fall into that self-focused survival mode that demands murder without remorse. Suffering dehumanizes. *Human* life is demanding in a different sense than the demands of heroic might and valor.

Human life is accomplished through the "thinking" that situates subjects, always already absorbed within their individual self-interested hedonisms, on the hitherside of their "ontologi-

---

1 Levinas, Otherwise Than Being, 185.

cal adventures," treading the difficult but rare path of a certain "shuddering weakness"—a "virility without cowardice." Living humanly leaves one, while still a "living being," "thinking" of the others that surround her—apprised of the suffering, hearing the cries of others with equal and perhaps greater needs. "Thought begins with the possibility of conceiving a freedom external to my own."[1]

Thinking sets the stage for the occurrence of the good, but it is not itself that event. Goodness still befalls the agent in the midst of ongoing projects, closed up in an egoistic world. The Good still possesses me, obsesses me, incarcerates me to its demand; it still calls for a courage I cannot muster and levies a debt that bankrupts my resources. One remains utterly passive in the occurrence of the good. But Levinas suggests that one can actively cultivate the passivity that awaits the arrival of the needy other. This cultivation begins in a "relaxation of essence."

To relax the inter-*esse* of living being's essence, the hero would not merely have to lay down his weapons and show the greater courage of resisting the urge to violence. He would need to resist the comfortable disposition toward mere life and actively cultivate the human life, even at the great risk of "thinking" where thought can be risky business, such as amongst prison guards and *kapos*, where beastliness abounds. Between *Totality and Infinity* and *Otherwise than Being*, Levinas recognizes that a "thinking being" must not only welcome the stranger and play "host" to the lonely wayfarer. He must assume responsibility even for the irresponsibility of other, more dangerous passers-by—heroes and other enraged torturers who delight in the crushing of innocents. Throwing open the doors of the domicile, the truly virile must lay at risk their solitary security, their meaningful existences, and the ideals of manly courageous action that have configured Western lifeworlds for thousands of years.

For Levinas, the "just war waged against war" is about overcoming a history of morally bankrupt standards that have configured the world for war. That history has left the survival of widows, orphans, and aliens to the might of the powerful heroes, but, as Agamemnon has shown, the heroic code of ethics

---

1 Levinas, Collected Philosophical Papers, 28.

dictates that the spoils of battle invariably go to the mightiest. To set the moral conditions for thoughtful existence that will question the moral standards of heroes and permit an escape of our egoisms into their full humanity, we must resist the triumphant theatrical pose that sees courage in acts of war. The "just war waged against war" is about the putting down of guns, the resisting of the seductive rebounding of violence. It is about the cultivation of higher ideals, more virile than the virility of the Greek hero. The war of heroic life is fought on an ideological terrain that positions us for aggressive response. To heroes and other warriors Levinas refuses to leave the question of justice.

Greek pride in virile action still guides our actions in the world. Superheroes still swoop down from the heavens, to set to rights an evil world. We hear constantly today of unambiguous "good guys" fearlessly hunting down unambiguous "bad guys." Again and again, politicians and militarists surface in front of us, on our television screens, to engage the patriotic fervor of their public, hoping to whip the terrorized and angry mob into a frenzy of vengeance and bloodlust. Few would blame the American people for their deep sense of outrage after the World Trade Center catastrophe. The incalculable damage is more than financial, more than the thousands of innocent lives, but has taken too people's sense of security and freedom. But unambiguous innocence even in victims of great offences can only be justly claimed so long as their reaction does not repeat the original crime.

But who is unambiguously good? Warriors against Western imperialism snuff out lives daily around the globe; Western warriors track terrorist foes through their rocky lairs and destroy them. Each side claims moral right. Each side claims victory. These wars have split the world in two, a clash of civilizations that is nothing less than murder *en masse* for hundreds of thousands of innocent civilians, as well as for innocent young men and women drafted into the war effort on both sides of the conflict. A mere gloss over the past centuries of Western history can give the "thinking" person pause to suspect the good intentions of the current wars. The current war rides on a logic deeply embedded in the Western world, the ethnocentric heroic logic that drove historical imperialisms and culminated in slavery, death camps, and holocaust.

It is important that we recognize that, while nations are composed largely of innocent civilians, no nation is an innocent party in the arena of world affairs. All nations have closeted skeletons. All states potentially repress and suppress their own, to greater or lesser degrees. The domain of violence in any society coextends with the over-determined assembly of powers and forces that configure it. It is not simply that each person succumbs to moral degradation under extremities of suffering and humiliation (as Holocaust survivors like Primo Levi and Elie Wiesel have repeatedly exposed). Abjection takes many forms in a universe so morally diverse. Perhaps, like the brave Achilles, we cannot see past our rage over past humiliations. It is imperative that we ask ourselves: is the hero's call for war the cry for justice, is it simply lust for enemy blood or for global power, or is the call to war simply motivated by the desire for booty that rewards all murderous armies? These darker possibilities seem inhuman but, as Levinas has insisted, humanity opens in the "thinking" that steps outside the arena of war, outside "allergic egoisms."

Over-serious nationalisms, myopic and incestuous tribalisms, and religious fundamentalisms flood the globe in the modern era. Claims of innocence and historical injustice are invariably accompanied by unambiguous and highly theatricalized condemnations of others. It is the condemnations themselves that depend on a sustained and orchestrated refusal to recognize that violence is not external to the global social fabric but constitutive of it. What is diabolical is not that each of us recognizes evil in the neighbor, but that we believe that the moralizing gesture of the witnessing grants expiation from the crimes of our heroes.

The stark fact of the matter is that evil is a rather common phenomenon. It comes to us in famine, flood, hurricane, childbirth, ageing, sickness, and death. And it comes to us in war. We can do little to remedy most of the evils that befall us, but we can remedy those few that come about as a result of the twisted heroic ideals that underlie our actions in the world and dictate vengeance upon "monstrous others" from purified seats of innocence.

CHAPTER SIX. EVIL IN NOMOS

Investigations into the religious and cultural lifeworlds of early human communities come to us through the disciple of anthropology, whose scholars study the *logos* (story or account) of *anthropos* (humankind) or *nomos* the cultural and religious traditions) of diverse human societies. Anthropology issued from its elder, more "grounded" (literally and metaphorically) cousin, archaeology. The anthropologist conjectures about the ways of life practiced by the earliest human beings whose relics the archeologist unearths. Anthropologists base their theories about religion and culture on the bones, burial grounds, weapons, tools, and artifacts discovered at archeological digs. They combine this information with investigations of modern tribal peoples, living in small-scale, simple societies in remote "uncivilized" areas.

1. Cautions Concerning Religious Anthropology

Anthropologists, historically, accompanied explorers and colonialists as they expanded their various empires across the globe. Thus their discipline could hardly avoid sharing the ethnocentric imperialist worldview of their host adventurers. This association colored anthropological ideas about the tribal peoples they encountered. Like the colonial adventurers, early anthropologists shared popular social Darwinist pseudo-scientific prejudices and assumed all human beings would evolve in similar ways until they eventually reached the summit of civilization and became like white Europeans. So anthropologists tended to name the strange exotic cultures "primitive" (ahistorical, unevolved since earliest human times). In fact, as late as 1965, E. E. Evans-Pritchard exposes his ethnocentric prejudice when he laments to his fellow anthropologists: "It is a remarkable fact that none of the anthropologists whose theories about primitive religion have been most influential have ever been near a primitive people."[1]

This categorical lumping together of the observable present with the long dead past lent justification to imperial projects of slaughter, enslavement, and exploitation of simple, indigenous societies, and expropriation of their land and resources. In importing the god and "civilization" to the "primitive" peoples of the earth, their invaders could claim to be the redeemers instead of murderers. The assumption that simple tribal peoples were identical to the earliest ancestors of the human species, unchanged over the millennia of European cultural evolvement, led the famed adventurer-explorer, Sir Samuel Baker, knighted for his (altogether faulty[2]) contribution to knowledge about primitive life, to declare before the *Ethnological Society of London*, in regard of modern tribal societies:

> Without any exception, they are without a belief in a Supreme Being; neither have they any form of worship or idolatry; nor is the darkness of their minds enlightened by even a ray of superstition. The mind is as stagnant as the morass which forms its puny world.[3]

We now know this assessment of simple indigenous peoples to be altogether faulty.[4] However, the prejudice against simple societies in which anthropology indulged for centuries was not

1 E. E. Evans-Pritchard, *Theories of Primitive Religion*, London: Oxford University Press, 1965.
2 Ibid., 7, n.2.
3 S. W. Baker, "The Races of the Nile Basin" in *Transactions of the Ethnological Society of London*, N.S.V (1867), 231, cited in Evans-Pritchard, Ibid., 6-7.
4 See Wendy C. Hamblet, *Savage Constructions: The Myth of African Savagery* (Amsterdam: Editions Lexington Books, 2004).

a peculiarity restricted solely to their discipline. Philosophers of the era were equally guilty of this damaging ethnocentrism. The French philosopher Lucien Lévy-Bruhl played an important role in persuading scholars of his day that the "primitive mentality" was fundamentally different—inferior not simply by way of quantity of "grey matter" but qualitatively inferior—in comparison to the mentality of the "civilized" modern European. The "primitive mentality" is more "mystical" and therefore "primitive" behavior is impossible to interpret in terms of individual psychology.[1] For Lévy-Bruhl, the mentality of any person is shaped in terms of the "collective representations" of society; individual representations re-present shared mental worlds that mirror the communal institutions peculiar to the social structure. Thus the scholar would need to understand the society's collective mental world in order to understand how individual thoughts were molded within that framework. Since institutions evolve over time, and since "primitive" peoples were granted no historical time, "primitive" mental worlds were deemed fundamentally different—backward, unevolved, irrational, illogical—in relation to Europeans.

Because of his very narrow thinking through a very broad lens, Lévy-Bruhl comes to categorize all human societies in two expansive groups: the civilized and the primitive. These two types represented, for Lévy-Bruhl, two radically opposed forms of thought, different not simply in degree but different in qualitative ways. Europeans, he contended, their historical worlds paved by centuries of rigorous intellectual labor, have developed reasonable patterns of thought and behavior; they are logically oriented and seek the reasons for things and events in natural causality according to scientific method. "Primitive" thought, on the other hand, is always entangled in supernatural explanations for things. Lévy-Bruhl states: "Objects and beings are all involved in a network of mystical participations and exclusions. It is these which constitute its texture and order."[2] Civilized minds

---

1 Lucien Lévy-Bruhl, *Primitive Mentality*, Lilian A. Claire, trans. (London: Allen & Unwin and New York: MacMillan, 1923); *The Notebooks on Primitive Mentality*, Peter Rivière, trans. (New York: Harper & Row, 1975).
2 Lucien Lévy-Bruhl, *Primitive Mentality*, 17-18.

fly to science for explanation of phenomena; primitive minds fly to the magico-religious and categorize things as manifestations of the occult. This difference leads Lévy-Bruhl to name "civilized" Europeans "logical" and "uncivilized" primitives "pre-logical."

I open this discussion of primitive religion with this small sketch of the history of anthropological and philosophical prejudice to demonstrate how carefully the scholar must tread in regard of her categorizations and speculations, how easily one might go astray unaware of one's own inherent prejudices against alien others. Much misery and slaughter has been levied upon simple tribal peoples because of the prejudice that claims that modern tribal peoples live and think like our human ancestors of millennia ago. This prejudice sets in motion a bias against the rational ability of tribal peoples.

We must admit candidly that we know very little about how the first human societies lived, thought, worshipped, raised their children, esteemed their elderly, and appeased their god(s). But we do know that many of the speculations about modern tribal peoples have shown themselves, with time and further study, to be altogether faulty. And we can be certain, from the mere longevity of their social forms and from the plethora of their cultural artifacts—art, music, natural medicines, intricate patterns of exchange, social intercourse with their neighbors, and stable, peaceful, highly-democratic political frameworks—that "simple" indigenous communities were not so "simple" after all and, in many respects, are superior to the bellicose and hostile Europeans who were overrunning them. We can also be certain that, with the ethno-religious fragmentation of the human world evidenced by third millennia warfare and the erosion of humanistic and holistic values caused by industrialization, urbanization, and global trade policies, Westerners have little *moral* evidence to prove their evolutionary superiority over simple indigenous peoples.

2. The Religious Worldview

Evil is a mythological image traditionally set in what is commonly called a religious worldview, i.e., a view of the world as the setting for grand narratives where cosmic forces of good and evil are played out across the epochs of historical time. The mythological explanatory model provides a common foundation for most religious communities, even the religion of atheism. Its stark imagery is popular because it is highly functional, especially during times of social crisis, because the religious worldview erects clear boundaries between polarized identities—good and evil. Stark, radically-polarized worldviews simplify life for believer communities, by plainly mapping out the terrain of social engagement: dividing what is prescribed from what is prohibited, what is loved by the god from what is not, and what respects from what transgresses the lawful boundaries of human practice and divinely-ordained justice. Evil occurs as the protagonist in the religious narrative, because it represents every feature that humans find unnerving: evil is unordered, undisciplined, unreasonable, incomprehensible by human cognitive powers. Evil is understood as a general principle that is despised not merely within the particular worldview, but by all that is decent and human.

3. The Archaic Roots of Religion

I have noted at the opening of this chapter that much anthropological theory concerning the religious and cultural roots of human societies was gleaned from observation of modern tribal peoples. Because of this faulty grounding equation, much of what is considered anthropological fact is little more than fiction. The scholar must proceed with exceeding humility, taking special care with sources, to confirm that anthropological speculations fit with archaeological evidence. One must rigorously employ a language of mindful conjecture rather than one of historical fact. To avoid the anthropological/philosophical trap of equating earliest human societies with modern tribal peoples, I shall confine myself to the research of those scholars whom Evans-Pritchard bemoans as "armchair scholars" who have never been near a "primitive" (as indeed no one of us today can do in any case, except by visiting the sites of archaeological digs).[1] I shall offer the following account of early human communities as a humble tale, a kind of speculative narrative or fanciful yarn,

---

1 E. E. Evans-Pritchard, *Theories of Primitive Religion*, 9.

whose truth cannot be claimed securely but whose "likely story" might provide insights into the roots of religious beliefs and cultural practices in use today.[1]

When the first of our species crawled out from the primeval forest, stood upright, and walked across the savannah, anthropologists speculate that they became, in one fell swoop, both more violent to alien groups and more nurturing of their own.[2] About fifty millennia before the Common Era, clans of our ancestors began to develop culturally, in leaps and bounds with the domestication of fire that permitted them warmth, cooked foods, protection from predatory animals, and fire-hardened tools and weaponry. There is strong evidence to suggest that these earliest clan-folk only stopped killing (and possibly eating) each other when the hunting of large carnivores necessitated that they focus their collective aggressive energies on the prey, instead of wasting them on internal rivalries.[3]

The prehistoric hunt was a rich moment in cultural development for early human communities, according to Walter Burkert. Over time in response to anxieties about killing and being killed and to meet the challenges of organization for the killing of deadly carnivores, a full palette of ritual life blossomed into existence, and rigorously-regulated practices cropped up to oversee every aspect of the hunt. These rituals compose the first signs of human religious life. Before-hunt rituals seduced

1 Socrates claims that the best humans can hope to achieve is a likely story. Plato, *Timaeus* 29cd. Socrates agrees with Timaeus' preamble to his account of the birth of the world: "As Being is to becoming so is truth to belief" and so "Enough if we adduce probabilities as likely as any others" and "we ought to accept the tale which is probable and inquire no further."
2 Dudley Young, *Origins of the Sacred; The Ecstasies of Love and War* (New York: St. Martin's Press, 1991), xix. Konrad Lorenz, writing in the 1960's, takes a darker view of human origins, naming aggression as primal to nurturing rituals, and love and friendship as "secondary rituals" developed from rituals of appeasement or redirected aggression. Konrad Lorenz. *On Aggression.* Marjorie Kerr Wilson, trans. (New York: Harcourt, Brace and World, 1966).
3 Walter Burkert offers the idea of the Paleolithic Hunt as the site of the birth of earliest religious and sacrificial ritual life. Creation of the Sacred: Tracks of Biology in Early Religions. Cambridge, Mass.: Harvard University Press, 1996; Homo Necans: An Anthropology of Ancient Greek Sacrificial Ritual and Myth. tr. Peter Bing. Berkeley: University of California Press, 1983; Structure and History in Greek Myth and Ritual. Berkeley, Calif.: University of California Press, 1979.

the prey into the hunting area, invoked the relevant spirits for their blessing (so that the animal, and not the hunters, would meet their end), focused communal vigor, and relieved anxieties spurred by the highly emotionally-charged event. During the hunt, the necessity of a clear hierarchical chain of command and a full set of organizational strategies required rigorous ranking and ordering of hunters and their shared painstaking attention to tactical detail. Post-hunt rituals defused aggressive anxieties, re-enacted the event for those who had remained at the hearth, and celebrated (or mourned) and set into ritual and oral histories the deeds of the brave hunters, as well as the formidable prowess of the enemy-prey.

Post-hunt festivities also called forth spirit blessings upon the booty of the hunt—the meat. "Proper" distribution of the booty reconfirmed (or altered as appropriate) the established political networks. Food distribution also confirmed the rankings of socio-economic status among the community at large, deciding and reflecting social realities, who properly belonged and who did not. Post-hunt festivals shaped the power configuration within the group and established "appropriate" patterns of interaction. The feast, song, dance, and communion with the spirits that the ritual celebration afforded the group reunified and revitalized the community, and confirmed the rightness of the status quo of power relations.

With time, the logical and symbolic ambiguities of the hunt would be addressed and negotiated through ritual as well, as it dawns on the group that the very animal they seek to kill is the same spirit they are enticing into the hunting area. God-spirit and animal are discovered as one, life-giving totem to the community. With this identification, ritual life expands to include the necessary apologies and purifications so that the dark deed of murder of a sacred entity becomes the willing *self*-sacrifice of a spirit-creature. The ritual observances of the community are the worship-payments demanded by the god-spirit-animal. The fact that the gods eventually come to be seen to "need" (or at least desire) the sacrifices from their human supplicants is evidenced in *The Hymn to Demeter*. In this ancient poem, Zeus intervenes to convince harvest-goddess Demeter to allow spring to return to earth so that humans do not die off, because the gods desire sacrifices.[1]

Rituals of sacrifice murder include human victims. In societies that worship a mother goddess, rites tend to be focused upon fertility of crops and human babies. Kings, queens, children, and babies as well as animals met with this ritual fate. Dionysian cults were known to tear apart animals, babies, and each other, in orgiastic festivals. René Girard claims murder-sacrifice rituals to have been pervasive of early human communities and sees them being re-enacted across the plethora of artistic forms.[2]

Murder-sacrifice rituals deserve our concerned attention because, contrary to popular belief, ritual predates myth by millennia and has a persistence that outlives it. As Dudley Young confirms, "ritual runs on automatic pilot, while myth without ritual runs on half-power at best."[3] There is clear evidence from archaeological finds that human beings enjoyed an abundant ritual life long before they developed the physiological equipment that permitted them speech. Myth composes the colorful depictions that arise to articulate the social knowledge that ritual had previously communicated from generation to generation through bodily participation—torture, expulsion, murder, sex, dance, and feast. Many anthropologists believe that, since violent rituals of murder-sacrifice (of human victims as well as animal) were practiced pervasively in the early millennia of human time, there is good reason to suspect that deep urges in the direction of murder are buried deep in our "civilized" flesh, waiting to spring forth the moment we feel threatened by a chaotic home-space or an alien presence.

Another important anthropological voice is that of Paul

---

1 Demeter is the goddess of the harvest, controller of the seasons and thus capable of destroying all life on earth. The central myth of Demeter, at the heart of the Eleusinian Mysteries, is Demeter's relationship with her daughter, Persephone. Persephone became the consort of Hades, the underworld god, when Hades abducted her from the earth. Demeter was so brokenhearted that she stopped the seasons and the harvest, so the human race was dying out. Zeus intervened to force Hades to bring Persephone back from the underworld, which he agreed to do for half the year, so that humans would survive and the gods would receive their sacrifices. Despite Plato, *Laws* 10.905d & ff.; 908e; 4.716e; 10.885d; 888c; 12.948; *Rep.* 2.364b & ff.
2 René Girard, *Violence and the Sacred*, Patrick Gregory, tr. (Baltimore: Johns Hopkins University Press, 1979).
3 Dudley Young, *Origins of the Sacred*, xxxv.

Radin, who contends that primitive religion arises as a function of cosmological inquiry, as "a mechanism devised by man for determining and evaluating the interrelationship between him and the external world."[1] The relationship with the earthly environment was surely one of extreme fear, on account of the economic and bodily insecurity that archaic life had to comprise for earliest human communities. A sense of extreme powerlessness and insignificance were bound to develop under these severe conditions for survival, and, Radin conjectures, "all this naturally led to a disorientation and disintegration of the ego [whose] mental correlate...is subjectivism."[2] Extreme subjectivism in the absence of "scientific" answers for confusing phenomena in the environment attributed coercive power to threatening objects in the surroundings, which in turn found expression in religious activity, with the dominance of magic, especially coercive rites and prescriptive/ prohibitive observances, to tame the threatening environment and to charm the local spirits into benevolence toward the community.

The earliest religious power figures, Radin speculates, may have been epileptics whose thrashing fits and strange speech-noises during seizures might have suggested to observers that the person was communicating with spirits or entering another dimension of reality. Since early priestly figures were likely well supported by their social group, in time a "profession" of those with special powers of mediation with the spirit world would have been established, a profession that grew lucrative and prestigious enough that it would have eventually attracted the healthy student (non-epileptic). There would have arisen religious cults and formal practices in magic in the form of apprenticeships that taught initiates the secrets of supernatural mysteries and the arts of coercive spirit-charms.

It is interesting to note that Radin refuses to claim any intellectual advantage of Westerners over our early ancestors, the pre-scientific age peoples. "All people," asserts Radin, "are spontaneously religious at crises...the markedly religious people are spontaneously religious on numerous other occasions as well, and...the intermittently and indifferently religious are second-

---

1 Paul Radin, *Primitive Religion*, New York: Dover, 1937, 3.
2 Ibid., 7.

arily religious on occasions not connected with crises at all."[1] Radin's assertion here is meant as a rebuttal to Lévy-Bruhl's ethnocentrism. Radin charges Lévy-Bruhl with a "fundamental error" in positing a "pre-logical mentality" in primitive folk over against the "scientific" rationality of the "civilized." Rather, claims Radin, we must recognize that different types of individuals at different times in their lives exhibit different types of thinking. In a most generous passage, Radin states:

> Had M. Lévy-Bruhl recognized the presence of these different types of individuals, I feel confident that he would never have postulated either a prelogical mentality or a mystical participation as the outstanding traits of all primitive thinking and that he would never have been led into the strange error of denying the existence, among primitive groups, of individuals who think as logically as do some of us and who are found alongside of others as irrational as are so many of us."[2]

Dudley Young, in his *Origins of the Sacred*, sets out from a yet another angle to unearth the secrets of the primitive mind and establish the grounding roots of religious encounter.[3] Young is convinced that the reality-altering phenomenon of religion must have arisen to address the paradoxes and contradictions that accompany the dynamics of sex and power in early human communities. Beginning millions of years in the past of human time, from the transformation of the arboreal monkey into the chimpanzee, Young explores the evolution of the naked ape in regard of the two factors of power and sex. From the time the first of our predecessors walked out of the primeval forest, stood upright and loped across the savannah, two things simultaneously changed: he became more violently aggressive in his hunting methods and he became more nurturing to his family and clan, and especially protective of the young. The greater hunting skill meant the greater consumption of meat which resulted in great increase in the human brain size and complexity of function. But the greater brain would have been more adept at recognizing

---

1 Ibid., 11. Emphasis mine.
2 Ibid., 12.
3 D. Young, *Origins of the Sacred*.

the paradoxes of the human condition, giving rise to socializing, "humanizing" responses to that condition. The simultaneous development of love and nurturing routines alongside the violent practices composing the hunt rituals demonstrates that these early people were changing in ambiguous ways—marking out the boundaries of belonging from non-belonging, developing a sense of social duty, and mapping out the laws and rituals that would regulate appropriate behaviors.

Young contends that the simultaneous urge to kill and to nurture would have occasioned the first experiences of "evil" in the community, necessitating the prohibitions and prescriptions that would regulate the killing impulse and restrict its discharge in the home community. Young attributes special importance to the role of the female of the species in (dare we say) civilizing the male. The essentially feminine rituals of mourning when killing was misdirected would have subtly persuaded the males to take care with their aggressive urges. Harm is for enemies; protection is for friends. The gods would have decreed it thus.

The rich palette of ritual life evidenced in archaeological finds Young attributes to this conceptually provocative era when the energies of the group were focused upon understanding the ambiguities of life and death, again dating this crucial phase about the time of the domestication of fire (50,000 years B.C.E.). Coercive ritual (magic) and, over time, the mythical articulations of these rites carved out the religious experiences of earliest human groups whereby they sought to charm the coercive spirits into benevolence and gift-giving. Myth and ritual developed into the "grammar of primitive experience," that "allow[ed] us to talk to the gods without being swallowed by them."[1] The big-brained primate needed to make sense of human life, a mysterious phenomenon that both knows its mortal limits and knows that it is alone, among the creatures of the earth, in recognizing this peculiar knowledge. In order to make reasonable this mystery, humans needed to instigate a narrative of beginnings in order to map out where their lives ought to proceed, and toward what ends. This task requires the permission of the gods, consecrated forms of god-friendly existence. A sacred time and place must be

---

1 Ibid., xx.

cordoned off from the chaos of mundane life.

Voila! The framework of the religious worldview takes shape, its ritual re-enforcements established and its mythical articulations spun. Hereafter existence and its myriad forms will be structured in two's—the sacred and the mundane; the good and the evil; the blessed and the cursed; the ordered and the chaotic. In centuries to come new two's would be added—the noble and the ignoble, the natural and the unnatural, the wise and the ignorant, the savage and the civilized.

Perhaps the most renowned, if controversial, of the anthropologists of violence is René Girard. His seminal work, *The Violence and the Sacred*, is meant to establish that religion composes the concealment *par excellence* of the violence that constitutes and is endemic to human community.[1] By separating the sacred home space off from the threatening chaos of the alien, religion provides the ritual means to project the aggressive urges of the community onto a stranger or neighboring community, so that cycles of internalized violence will not plague the home community with what Girard names a "sacrificial crisis." In a troubling universal move, Girard locates the scapegoat mechanism at the heart of each and every artistic artifact and cultural development of human communities throughout time.

Today most religious believers understand their religion to compose the very arena wherein the spiritual life takes shape, where the ethical demands of the god may be deciphered from historical wisdoms set down in ritual ceremony and sacred text, interpreted by a divinely ordained priestly leader, and communicated to the congregation. Thus and perhaps only thus is the god's plan understood to have hope of being realized. Thus and only thus might the ethically-structured spiritual life emerge—in community with others sharing the self-defining belief system, each equally concerned to fulfill the divine dictates of the moral life.

However, if it is true, as the anthropologists claim, that religion is an invention of human communities to regulate the aggressive urges, sublimating them or redirecting them onto unsuspecting innocents within the community or neighboring to

---

1 Girard, René. *Violence and the Sacred.*

it, then we might expect to find in modern religious forms traces of the demonization mechanism, the process that projects communal evil onto alien others, along with other concealed formulae and symbols that legitimate violence. We might expect to find, encoded in the sacred practices and texts that lend identity and solidarity to the religious group, the holy summons to sacrifice (and especially the ultimate self-sacrifice—the religious war upon infidels), the two-worlds view of reality (sacred and profane), and the notion of evil as an alien contaminant (infecting the sacred community from without) or as a creative confusion within the god-concept (as the angry, judgmental "other face" of the god). Looking upon the world today and witnessing the Cain-like fervor with which zealots of each of the three "World's Great Religions" (though spawned from one and the same father, Abraham) meet each other's differences, it is easier to believe that modern religions remain faithful to religion's sacrificial origins, than it is to believe that religion inspires moral life and a sense of the sacredness of life. Illuminating those danger zones where believers may morally slip in regard of their own moral ideals will be the next task of this segment of the current work.

4. Moral Fault-lines in the Religious Worldview

Religion has often been named, by cultural anthropologists and violence researchers, as the archaic "root of violence." René Girard is one of the most vocal proponents of this view, but Girard's theory of "violence and the sacred" culminates in a confirmation of the Christian faith as the one religion that, in arising from the *self*-sacrifice of the sacred savior figure, disarms the inherent chaotic violence generally associated with religion. To make this case, Girard distinguishes between the "bad violence" that spirals out of control from psychological forces founded in mimetic rivalry and the "good violence" of appropriate religion.

According to Girard, religion is "good violence" because it channels the aggressive urges of the society toward an innocent third party "scapegoat" for the "good" purpose of discharging those dangerous but inevitable energies which would otherwise overflow in a societal bloodbath en masse. Without the "good violence" of religion, claims Girard, a "sacrificial crisis" would occur in which all people in the society would struggle in a life and death battle over the shared "love-objects" after which they commonly lust.

The scholar of violence is encouraged by the frank connection Girard forges between violence and all things sacred. It is clear from this believer's account, as from the evidence of long histories of church-sponsored tortures, witch-burning campaigns, crusades against alien religious sects, tyrannical church-run political regimes, the hushing of sexual abuse scandals, cruel educational and punishment practices, church complicity in Nazi extermination projects, imperialistic endeavors and colonial projects, that religion lends itself quite readily and easily to wanton violences that are difficult to categorize by anyone's standards as "good."

On the other hand, religious leaders have proven tireless and selfless in their devotion to the cause of human rights in the world. Martin Luther King, Mahatma Gandhi, Mother Teresa, Desmond Tutu, and Archbishop Romero have, in the name of their gods, spoken out loudly and publicly and at great peril to their own lives, in favor of the wretched of the earth. Churches have long supported the disenfranchised and the oppressed; they have provided (and continue in much of the world to provide) sanctuary for the pursued and disenfranchised, meeting places for the budding unions of the demoralized and exploited workers of the third world, and medical services to the otherwise forgotten and educational opportunities in the most remote reaches of the planet. Churches have housed and funded projects the world over that sought to improve the lot of the lowliest among us.

Religion's other-facing *ethos* demands tireless attendance upon the widowed, the orphaned and the alienated. It counsels an overcoming of the modern focus upon the vapid pleasures of the material world, and an attention to human suffering in concrete works. In fact, for centuries the single only charity houses and welfare systems available to the impoverished were to be found in the local churches. If the religious worldview, whatever the religion in question, could/would be realized on planet earth, surely the planet would be greatly improved and the entire human species more secure, sheltered in familial embrace. It is beyond doubt that religion provides human beings a point of entry to the spiritual dimension of existence that gives access onto the moral life.

In the loftiness of their theoretical bases, churches claim their religion to be a force for peace and human siblinghood. But in practice, religion has often sounded the war cry that has culminated in some of the worst crimes against humanity. Thus arises the compelling question: What is it about religion that compromises its lofty ideals? There must exist deep structural flaws in the religious worldview, "moral fault-lines" through which the morally weak, the fanatical, and the unscrupulous justify their violences. The religious worldview must be riddled with moral "gaps" through which believers can slip into radical evil. This paper attempts to illuminate some of the dangers embedded in the conceptual parameters that form the horizons of the religious worldview and to demonstrate how these danger sites can come to legitimate the evil they promise to battle in the world, the evil that religious disciples of most faiths would readily condemn in others.

5. The Phenomenon of Religious Experience

William James, in *Varieties of Religious Experience*, articulates the problem of fairly judging an alleged "religious experience" from outside of the experience itself. James explains that the *mysterium tremendum* of contact with a superhuman being would likely compose an experience that defies expression to others. The signs may be quite visible—one might stammer and stutter, faint, cry out, or speak "in tongues"—but the onlooker would have no tools to measure the authenticity of the experience from witnessing the event itself.[1]

No, concludes James, one could only be certain that a religious experience had actually occurred if one could mark a radical change in the person after the religious event. James reasons that being touched by the god would be so radically life-altering that, in the case of an actual religious experience, the experienc-

---

1 William James, *Varieties of religious Experience* (New York: Modern Library, 1994).

er's life would be altered forever. The change would be easily de-
tectable, according to James, by an analysis of the person's post-
event works. If post-event works were the work of a god—the
doing of good, the leading of the lost, the feeding of the hungry,
the offering of sanctuary to the pursued—we may be certain the
person has had an authentic religious experience.

Clearly, however, this is not always the case. From the wan-
dering Hebrews outside Jericho's walls to France's Joan of Arc,
sometimes the god is cited as inspiring his disciples to wage war
on his enemies. Many aspects of the religious experience must
exist that can cause violence rather than compassion to follow
contact with the god.

The first and most obviously dangerous element is to be located in the believer's view of the nature of the god. Certainly a
view of god as vindictive, jealous, angry, crusading, judgmental
and fearsome will effect in its followers like characteristics.

The earliest religions did not in fact need to invent an anti-
christ or evil demon; the god was seen as having dual faces. Like
the Roman god of the portal, Janus, the god looked kindly upon
friends and fiercely upon enemies. Thus, the Romans, like the
Greeks before them, understood power as duplicitous in aspect.
The old myths describing the events by which the gods brought
cosmos out of chaos were exceedingly violent. They employed
"ordering mechanisms" that include thunder bolts, lightning
spears, floods, plague and pestilence, wars and so on. However
violent the means the gods employ, their accomplishments are
always deemed unqualifiedly good. The problem with this view
of the god was noted by Plato (and this explains his dismissing
the poets from the just state of the *Republic*): a god that is good
does good, no matter whether he is rewarding friends or heap-
ing harm upon his enemies. Socrates noted the problem of a god
that sets his own rules for what is good when speaking with
Euthyphro in the Platonic dialogue of the latter's name. When
a thing is good because the god loves it, he can be called upon to sanctify any evil thing. On the other hand, if the god loves something
because it is good, the god submits his own desires to a higher
law. When the god refuses to conform to any external measure
of appropriate behavior, it is a short leap for disciples to do the
same, and in the name of their god.

Religious myths are often taken to render the deepest truths about human existence. In early myths, the monsters gods often appeared to test the moral and physical strength of the hero. Perseus slays Medusa, Hercules kills the Hydra, and Odysseus blinds the Cyclops. These heroes (the word hails from *eros*, meaning half-god or mediator between human and divine realms of existence), like the gods they model, perform monstrous deeds of vicious valor as testimony to their superhuman ontological status. Abraham, father of the three great religions of the world, is understood to have taken his young son to the verge of a bloody slaughter to please the whim of his god, never questioning the god on the justness of this act.[1] Job, a good man, was robbed of everything he valued, his family and all his possessions, by a god who also would not be questioned on his motives. "Where were you when I made heaven and earth?" he asks the poor man struggling to fathom the god's ambiguous justice.

On the other hand, if the structure of the cosmos were such that the gods fit the second model of Socrates' description, there would exist *absolute* measures of conduct beyond the whim and will of individual gods, rules of moral behaviors to be followed by all adherents including the god. Such a god would serve as a better exemplar for human emulation that the wicked, angry, haughty, jealous, judgmental gods of old tales. However, even this more morally restricted view of the god opens another fault-line at the feet of the would-be do-gooder. Absolute rules and absolute truths are deeply comforting to the adherent. They provide a clear blueprint for the blessed life. However, absolutes quickly harden into dangerous dogma that leaves little room for toleration of the differences of neighbors. With religion, much is marked as "sacred." That is, rules and beliefs are taken very seriously, as though emanating straight from the god (or through intermediary saints or ministers on earth).

Each religious group has its unique set of beliefs and rules to distinguish their identity group from other groups. It would not do if a religious sect matched identically with other systems. This uniqueness is good for the adherents, performing crucial "identity work" that permits them to name their desirable quali-

---

1 Carol Delaney, *Abraham on Trial* (Princeton, NJ: Princeton University Press, 2000).

ties "identity markers" that can be shared across the group. These markers of unique character allow adherents to develop self-esteem and a distinctive view of themselves. On the other hand, within the religious worldview, where these "identifying markers" are seen as established by the god or his powerful representatives on earth, it is easy for the home group to overvalue their own inflexible *absolute* dogma. Since that dogma is always morally-significant, it is equally easy, in the view of the home-group, for outside groups to come up morally wanting.

Much of what goes morally awry in the religious worldview is associated with this over-serious propensity for exclusive loyalty to the group and the concomitant exclusionism of otherness that results from an inwardly-turned, sickened exclusivity. If religions could really master the "catholicism" that they generally profess, then there would be greater hope for the realization of the universal love and peace that most religions profess to be seeking.

Another factor that can affect whether compassion or violence will follow religious experience is the size of the church as a power structure. Religions, like states, may find it possible to maintain peaceful community by nonviolent means only so long as their numbers remain quite dwarfed. Once any identity structure becomes a superstructure, a power entity of considerable size, it may be destined to take on dark aspects. Power corrupts, as Plato affirms, even in the most priestly and philosophical spirit. We may expect higher things of some spirits, but as historian Lord Acton's (1834–1902) epic warning recalls: "The danger is not that a particular class is unfit to govern. Every class is unfit to govern. Power tends to corrupt, and absolute power corrupts absolutely."

Churches of old, however benevolent their beginnings, quickly grew larger than could be managed by benevolent means. Furthermore, many of the early religions that now dominate the world scene themselves began in violence. Many, like the early Jews and Christians, had to struggle to survive the radical persecution of non-believers. Violence begets violence. The major religions of the world compose massive political structures and religious structures are structurally analogous to any power edifice in the world. Strong leadership and oppressive methods may be called into play to keep followers faithful to the will of the church leaders.

The ontological structure of churches can present a danger-ous example for its followers. Generally a strong male leader-ship governs absolutely and dictates hierarchical socio-political arrangements that are so profoundly tied up with wealth and political power that they are easily bent to illicit ends. Since the gods retired from the earth and took up their abode in a tran-scendental realm off in the heavens somewhere, the men placed in charge of communicating his messages to the world cannot be questioned on the authenticity of their claims.

When a church leadership (and, in these latter days, even secular leaders) rally religious discourse in favor of wars of ag-gression, it is difficult for simple pious folk to resist the seduc-tive language of "god's mission" and the meting of the god's justice to evildoers. The problem is that, though religions have fought long and hard to expel any Gnostic traces in their ranks, the religious worldview too readily lends itself to facile us/them good/evil oversimplifications of complex world events and peoples. Once good people hear the cry to fight evil in the name of the god, they are all too often quick on the scene with their pitchforks and their shotguns. Moral outrage and indignation tend to obsessions of sacredness in the faithful and illusions of unqualified self-righteousness. Under the influence of these emotive forces, violence against innocent others can be con-ducted in good conscience by the firmest believers in the golden mean and the golden rule. Human relations can turn ugly when the god's representatives are taken too seriously and individual consciences become clouded by persuasive rhetoric. Often the use of archaic long-dead language in church ritual, the exclusive interpretation of scripture, or the abstractness of religious no-tions forbid questioning by mere laypeople. Sacred symbols are taken up, conceptual as well as material, that seduce the simple believer to leave important moral questions to those best "in the know." Church rituals themselves often imply a taking in of vio-lence—the "blood and the flesh" of Christ—under the direction of a specially ordained leader sanctioned to carry out the deed. It is a small conceptual leap from the faithful drinking the blood of Christ to the spilling of enemy blood in the name of the god.

Much of religious ritual defies human reason. But, then, the defying of human reason is the whole point of religion in many people's worldview. Religion is called upon to make sense of the mysteries of life by referring them to the greater wisdom of the god. And tragedies of human existence can be submitted to the god's court for compensation in a transcendental gift system. "The meek shall inherit the earth." As Nietzsche has argued *ad nauseum*: the religious worldview elevates the slave mentality and crushes the life forces from people.[1] Nietzsche states: "The sick and perishing—it was they who despised the body and the earth, and invented the heavenly world, and the redeeming blood-drops...From their misery they sought escape"[2]

The promise of immortality, extended by most religious systems, composes a transcendental gift system that not only devalues the earth and the body with its "wayward" passions, impulses and emotions, but it renders payment after-the-fact for a miserable and slavish life that is makes a virtue of submission to wretchedness. This promise, like the notion of a divine plan or a divinely-determined destiny, serves in human politics to maintain the status quo of power relations. The downtrodden are opiated with these notions to put up with the social injustices that oppress them. *The god has all things in order, though men may not fully understand their wisdom at present, but all will be made right in the fulfillment of time when the lion lies down with the lamb.* Fyodor Dostoevsky, in the chapter of the Brothers Karamazov named "Rebellion," wrote at length about the ironies of a benevolent all-powerful architect of a divine plan within which ultimate happiness for all is purchased through the torture of little innocents. "Would you be the architect of such a plan?" the philosophical Ivan asks his monk-brother, Alyosha. "No, I would not," whispers the brother.

Another moral fault-line that has historically served, and continues to serve unscrupulous imperialistic enterprises and political agendas, as well as church evangelical projects, is the theory of history inherent within the religious worldview. Religions give meaning to people's suffering as an effective means

1 Friedrich Nietzsche, *Thus Spoke Zarathustra*, Part One, III, IV.
2 Nietzsche, *Thus Spoke* Zarathustra, Manuel Komroff, ed., (New York: Tudor, 1889), 28-29.

to their being brought unto the god. In the religious worldview, humankind is "fallen" from an archaic happy home with the god. The way back to the god's company is said to be difficult and thorny, but suffering serves in the salvation process. Suffering brought to the Africans in the abuse and humiliation of slavery and of colonial rule could be justified to the native folk as a salvational path to redeem them from their evil "god-less" past (though Africans were monotheistic before most of the Western world made that conceptual advancement).

Notions of evil as other to the "chosen" of the god have been rallied to justify all manner of slaughter and abuse throughout history. Being chosen by a god is certain to embolden a population to a haughty self-righteousness. Evil, in the religious worldview, is often expressed by the metaphor of disease. Evil is said to creep into a people or into an individual's heart like an insidious infection. In the distorted medical beliefs of past centuries, diseases were often "bled out" or the infected region cut out and the virus killed. This metaphor serves well in the rhetoric of holy war and continues to serve well today in promoting otherwise god-fearing people to enlist in wars of aggression against different others. Even the very criteria designed to restrict war, developed by Christian thinkers like St. Augustine and St. Thomas Aquinas, take as a grounding assumption that *some* wars are just and good. Though the prohibition against killing is a universal feature of every state and every religious group, there is quasi-universal acceptance of this assumption that some wars are condoned by gods and are thus justifiable to humans.

The revelation of these many fault-lines in the religious worldview are not meant to suggest that religion is nothing beyond a dangerous anachronism that needs to be overcome if the world is to move forward into peace. Too many undeniable benefits issue from the religious worldview, as the very cradle of the spiritual life of human beings and the wellspring of *karitas*. However, these moral fault-lines remind us that a church is a power structure of identity: it builds its uniqueness on the foundation of counter-cultural rejection and exclusion; it must demonize difference, if it is to carve out its pillars of unique sacredness.

The fact that churches compose power structures should warn us that a church—as any worldly entity that takes itself too seriously, that considers its dogma absolute and universally-applicable, that posits its governing truths closed to new interpretations, and holds its leaders as infallible as the god—runs a great risk of legitimating behaviors that most religious folk would, in others, condemn as "evil." We must recognize that all belief systems are of human making and are thus error-prone. They all reveal structural and ethical flaws over time and will need to be re-constructed again and again until they "get it right."

How can we know when we've got it right? William James has pointed the way. An authentic religious experience mandates life-promoting behaviors of a divine quality in the person so touched by the god. It is imperative that religious folk, as well as secular good people of the earth, keep "working at the horizons" of their lifeworlds, as the post-moderns say, checking to be sure that our works in the world hold as primary concern the welfare of the human family, not simply the particular religious fold.

6. Evil as the Other Face of the God(s)

If cattle and horses or lions had hands and were able to draw with their hands and do the works that men do, horses would draw the forms of the gods like horses, and cattle like cattle, and they would make their bodies such as they each had themselves.[1]

Xenophon (431–355 BCE) certainly seems correct in his claim that humans invent gods in their own image. The gods of Hesiod and other ancient poets, before they come to be purified by Plato and, later, transcendentalized by Christianity, show every sign of being cut from the same morally challenged fabric as their human inventors. The gods of the ancients are depicted as fully representative of the extreme possibilities of evil and good that we find in human beings. The Olympians display all the troublesome qualities that Plato reserves for human souls alone.[2]

---

1 Fragment 15, Clement Strom. V, 109, 3, as cited in G. S. Kirk, J. E. Raven, *The PreSocratic Philosophers*, Cambridge, Mass.: Cambridge University Press, 1957), 169.
2 *Phaedrus* myth of the fall 242a-249a.

Zeus himself is promiscuous and driven nomadically by his wanton desires, infamous among gods and men for his lusty seductions of goddess, as often as unwary human lass. Hera, enraged at each new escapade, seems not to care in the least whether the unhappy damsel has been a deceived or willing consort, but blindly levies a cruel vengeance against her husband's trophies. The gods of the ancient Greeks indulge in every sort of indiscretion that, later, Christianity, will come to call "sins." The gods of the ancient Greeks are morally two-faced. They are naughty and they are nice. Zeus, king of the Olympian pantheon, is quick to punish a cruel injustice or to avenge a slighted friend; he is equally quick to don the guise of a creature and attack a poor human maiden.

The mischievous Greek gods do not merely levy evil on unsuspecting human victims; they seem to have decreed that humans themselves must partake in evil agency as well. Odysseus' tragic life exemplifies this hapless curse, as his cruel destiny is brought to fruition, not despite but precisely through the convoluted antics to which he extends himself in his efforts to avoid that fate. It is true that the gods do not outright deny human beings the "free will" whereby they might hope to escape their accursed lots, so that men cannot simply be construed as the innocent pawns of the gods. On the other hand, fate clearly follows each heroic figure about till it tips his own hand in the direction of the mal chance.

Another way of explicating the ironic, ethically-fated, morally-self-defeating "free will" that seems to be divinely allotted to humans is to employ the mythical metaphor: according to the ancient tales, Zeus gave men to choose their fate between two (at least to some degree) self-defeating urns. One urn is filled with bad luck and the other with a mixture of bad and good. Thus no human being, whatever her choices, can escape some degree of both ill luck and moral failure. The god's most favored hero seems but a plaything in the quarrels between the gods. The "best of the Achaeans" (Iliad VIII.73-82) are doomed to fall into petty dispute, earn their name in the ambiguous trade of life for fame (I.352-54), and achieve military triumph only at the cost of many a personal defeat and the loss of many a loved one. Priam and Achilles, grand masters among men, in many respects, seem more passive victim-recipients of Zeus' whims than masters of their own fate.

Sometimes, it seems that little more is at work in the universe than divine caprice, but John Alvis, in his *Divine Purpose and Heroic Response in Homer and Virgil*, asserts that Zeus dispenses providence according to four basic principles:

> (1) extraordinary divine endowments entail extraordinary costs; (2) men and women must abide the consequences of their own actions; (3) injustice must be checked; and (4) humans must observe usages...that acknowledge their difference from the gods.[1]

Whatever Zeus' own moral failings, he will suffer no unpaid moral debt from his ontological subordinates. If Zeus has a plan in regard of the human drama, it is to situate human beings in their rightful ontological position—between beast and god. Zeus falls with a cold vengeance upon humans who would elevate themselves to superhuman status. Zeus may manifest few rigid moral standards in his own affairs, but he is quick to punish *hybris* in the human world, whether in matters of state where great leaders fail to exercise befitting governance over their lessers, in the unjust treatment of enemies, in the proper reception and care of strangers, or in rendering suitable respect toward peers.

I have said that the Greek Olympians hold humans to higher standards than they themselves are willing to observe. However, it is equally true that the Olympians indulge in their vices without cruelty or malice. One might even say that, though the deities are personified, an impersonal methodical normative certainty, a kind of nemesis, follows upon their moral lapses. Even Zeus, according to the Hymn of Demeter, is bound to intervene and put right the wrongs of his divine brothers. Perhaps this is because the oldest of the gods are *Moira* (Fate), *Tukhē* (Honor), *Anankē* (Necessity) and *Dikē* (Justice). These four norms form the firm moral horizon against which the divine drama is played out.

No Greek or Roman god compares in duplicity with Janus,

1 John Alvis, *Divine Purpose and Heroic Response in Homer and Virgil*, Lanham, Maryland: Rowman & Littlefield, 1995. 13.

the Roman god of the doorway, patron of beginnings and end-ings. Janus steps down from the Roman pantheon into the per-manence of history as the exemplar *par excellence* of the double-dealing god. Above the great doors of the Roman Empire, closed but twice in the long hegemony of that great state, smiled and grimaced the god that welcomes friend and harmless wayfarer but terrifies the advancing enemy. Janus manifests in his split visage the ambivalence all people hold toward the stranger. The gods from time immemorial issued their decree that the stranger must be welcomed into our homes, be given a bed and a share in our foods. But the gods give no guarantee against the risks of that naive welcome. Homer, Plato, and Aristotle all remind us that the stranger can prove a god or a monster.[1] The cautious admit the unknown into their midst with, at best, a duplicitous reception.

7. The Gods Rise to Perfection; Humans Fall

Plato insists that the gods be purified, or rather, he holds that poets must stop telling lies about the gods.[2] Evil belongs to human souls; gods never morally falter. The distinction be-tween the perfect gods and morally faulty men is sketched out in the *Phaedrus* where gods and humans are depicted en route to a heavenly feast. Passing up the steep ascent in a gracious and orderly fashion, the gods step onto the great wheel of the heav-ens and are carried around to feast upon the various excellent aspects of Being—Being being'ly being. Excellence, in turn, is nurtured within them. They gaze upon the forms (*eidos*; pl. *eidoi*; from *eidenai*, having dual meanings: "to look" and "to know") and, as they consider the varied aspects of the good with the clear eye of the mind, they increase in moral knowing. With every "look," the souls grow increasingly like the virtuous forms they contemplate.

---

1 Homer, *Odyssey* 17.485 ff: *In the likeness of strangers [come the gods]*; Plato, *Republic* 2.381d; Aristotle. Strangers are gods and monsters in the kitchen.

2 *Phaedrus* 247a "for *phthonos* has no place in the heavenly choir." *Phthonos* is generally translated as "jealousy" but, in the full richness of the an-cient Greek language, the term is meant to depict every negative qual-ity of character that signals moral decay—covetousness, invidiousness, competitivism, acrimoniousness, malice, resentment, ill will, envy.

The *Phaedrus* myth depicting the fall of the soul from its original heavenly abode (246-249), Plato has Socrates tell what the human soul is like (since a "likely story" is the best that one may do in any case). Describing the human soul's struggle to ascend to ethereal heights alongside the godly train, Socrates tells that human souls have a far more difficult task than do the gods in rising to the Feast of Being, because human souls suffer from *phthonos*, a quality that the perfect gods do not share. *Phthonos* has no place amongst the heavenly choir but is the found in human souls alone. Its meanings are broad but always dark, embracing every negative feature associated with a gluttonous materialism—envy, ill will, invidiousness, voraciousness, malice, resentfulness, covetousness, acrimony, competitiveness, suspiciousness, and greed. Liddle and Scott end their rich array of meanings for this term with the nebulous characteristic, "heartburnings."

Human souls are so debilitated by these various unfortunate "heartburnings" that, instead of working in concert to achieve the steep ascent to the heavens, instead of following in an orderly choir in the manner of the gods themselves, human souls begin thrashing about and shoving and treading on one another. Human souls, in this dialogue imaged as two steeds and a charioteer, struggle against internal divisions among the reasonable charioteer, the impassioned white steeds of noble birth, and the ill-formed dark steeds of insatiable appetite. The steeds stomp and snort and trounce about, until the delicate wings that uplift them are shattered and broken from their sturdy frames. Wings lost, human hopes for perfection and happiness are lost too. Helpless and fragile, the soul flutters to the earth "until it can fasten on something solid" (246c). This tragic creature, embodied self-division, hopeless and broken, takes form again in a new earthly incarnation, "a living being and mortal" (246d).

Plato is concerned that the Greek gods serve as exemplars for human modeling. He attempts to purge the unruly heavenly host of the divine "evils" that they are seen to practice in Hesiod's *Theogony* and other old poems and hymns. It is important to note, however, that the Greek gods at their worst remind us more of naughty pranksters and playful children than malicious demons typical of the later Christian "devil" figures. The playfulness of Zeus and Poseidon, considered beside the jealous, capricious, and bloodthirsty Yahweh, one is challenged to wonder whether something important was lost when the gods become so all-fired serious—something important *to morality*. Nietzsche warns: Never to trust a god who doesn't dance!

8. Gods That Don't Dance

For an ancient god of severe, stern demeanor we may look to the ancient god of the Hebrew Bible (Christian "Old Testament"). This divine figure is no sentimental father-on-a-cloud. Rather, he manifests the full set of qualities that a later world will ascribe to a demon. Yahweh is a jealous, judgmental, humorless deity, every bit as vengeful, parochial, intolerant, and bigoted as the worst of human kings and megalomaniacs. Two tales exemplify the dark face of Yahweh, the stories of Job and Abraham.

Genesis 22:1-2 tells the story of Abraham and Isaac. In this tale, god orders Abraham to kill his only son Isaac, whom god has already identified as the seed and future of the Hebrew peoples. Without question, without explanation to his wife Sarah or his son, Abraham gathers the boy for the kill and takes him off to Mount Moriah where he prepares the altar of sacrifice. Only at the last moment does god free Abraham from the obligation by providing an alternative sacrificial victim.

God tested Abraham, and said to him, "Abraham!" And he said, "Here am I." He said, "Take your son, your only son Isaac, whom you love, and go to the land of Moriah, and offer him there as a burnt offering upon one of the mountains of which I shall tell you." So Abraham rose early in the morning . . . . When they came to the place of which God had told him, Abraham built an altar there, and laid the wood in order, and bound Isaac his son, and laid him on the altar, upon the wood. Then Abraham put forth his hand, and took the knife to slay his son. But the angel of the LORD called to him from heaven, and said, "Abraham, Abraham!" And he said, "Here am I." He said, "Do not lay your hand on the lad or do anything to him; for now I know that you fear God, seeing you have not withheld your son, your only son, from me." And Abraham lifted up his eyes and looked, and behold, behind him was a ram, caught in a thicket by his horns; and Abraham went and took the ram, and offered it up as a burnt offering instead of his son.

Theologians of all three religions spawned from Abraham (Jewish, Christian, and Muslim) have wrestled with this foundational story. Søren Kierkegaard's treatment of it in *Fear and Trembling* is considered seminal by philosophers. In Kierkegaard's account, Abraham comes off a great moral hero for his ability to set aside his personal misgivings to follow blindly a paradoxical order from god. Witness his "Eulogy on Abraham":

> There was one who relied upon himself and gained everything; there was one who in the security of his own strength sacrificed everything; but the one who believed God was the greatest of all. There was one who was great by virtue of his power, and one who was great by virtue of his hope, and one who was great by virtue of his love, but Abraham was the greatest of all, great by that power whose strength is powerlessness, great by that wisdom which is foolishness, great by that hope whose form is madness, great by the love that is hatred to oneself.[1]

For Kierkegaard, the story of Abraham is the archetypical narrative that demonstrates the inexpressible, incomprehensible, paradoxical nature of faith, and of the truest moral acts. Moral situations call people to do what is not always in their best interests. Moreover, faith by definition calls for trust in the face of the absurdness of that trust. Abraham cannot explain to others, and certainly not to his wife Sarah, the grave act he is about to perform. He has no explanation to offer. Both faith and moral acts are often like that: they are inexplicable, inexpressible to others. Yet at the same time, asserts Kierkegaard, the story of Abraham demands retelling: "and speak one must, from respect for greatness."[2]

The problem of expression and explication is centered around the problem of the limitations inherent in the epistemological tools of systematic philosophy. Georg Wilhelm Friedrich

---

1 Søren Kierkegaard, *Fear and Trembling* (London, Eng.: Oxford University Press, 1939), 117.
2 Ibid., 109.

Hegel, at every stage of the *Phenomenology of Spirit*, subsumes all epistemological challenges under a higher synthesis. But moral acts, shows Kierkegaard, are often acts of faith undertaken in an epistemological void over which knowledge cannot triumph. Moral acts are often simply absurd. "Personally, I have devoted a considerable amount of time to the study of Hegelian philosophy, and I believe I understand it fairly well.... On the other hand, whenever I try to think about Abraham, I am as it were annihilated."[1] Hegel's Absolute Spirit makes sense of everything over time, but what if moral acts refuse to be subsumed within their neat calculations of a sovereign Reason? Moral acts are acts of faith, which by definition remain nonsensical, inexplicable to self and others. The Abraham story "utterly astounds me and my brain twists and turns in its skull," the Dane declares[2]

Emmanuel Levinas, in his "The Trace of the Other," also sees Abraham as a kind of hero, and he uses the Abraham story as another kind of (morally-significant) archetype. In an obvious attempt to challenge the anti-Semitic prejudice that Jews are cowards, Levinas uses Abraham to epitomize a Jewish bravery that sets off into a wilderness, whose destination is unknown. Abraham's trek out of slavery in Egypt and across the forbidding desert, as well as Abraham's call to sacrifice his son on Mount Moriah, for Levinas represents a typical Jewish courage to go on in the face of absurd degrees of adversity. Abraham again becomes a paragon of moral right in Levinas' treatment, as the philosopher compares favorably the Jewish courage that has no comforting explanatory frame to the Greek adventurism of a Ulysses, who seems to be setting off into the great unknown but always seeks a safe return home, a return to the selfsame and not to a true other. The Greek hero typifies Western heroism, a lesser heroism than the Jewish, because Ulysses "through all of his peregrinations is only on the way to his native island."[3]

Abraham also epitomizes for Levinas the adventurism of Western philosophy. Like Kierkegaard, Levinas sees the journey of Ulysses as a model for the Western-Hegelian philosophy of

1 Ibid., 39.
2 Ibid., 68.
3 Emmanuel Levinas, "The Trace of the Other," *Deconstruction in Context*, Mark Taylor, ed. (Chicago: University Of Chicago Press, 1986), 348.

immanence that equates thought with being, a closed model of philosophy that successfully captures being within a subject's thinking, and within which the other emerges only as the transmutation of the same. Abraham demonstrates another kind of philosophy, a tradition seen in the Talmudic writings of the Jewish tradition, in which knowledge goes out to capture the other but is foiled. As in the Abrahamic journey, an absurd courage is required because the promised destination is unknown and the threat of unlimited sacrifice is ever present.

In *The Gift of Death*, Jacques Derrida too takes up the Abraham story, this time staging a typically Levinasian "face to face" encounter between Levinas and Kierkegaard.[1] Derrida, whose thought is deeply influenced by Levinas' heterology, takes up the question of the inexpressibility, exemplified by Abraham's experience on Mount Moriah, and proposes that inexpressibility ensures ethics. Ethics is a question of the secret. When moral acts are secrets, the purity of the moral act is ensured. Moral acts are pure gifts to the recipient because the secrecy that keeps the act hidden forbids the possibility of self-congratulations as well as forbidding the accolade of spectators who might influence the selflessness of the act by their approval and appreciation.

Abraham epitomizes the moral actor because god's reasons are secret from him, absurd in his calculations. Abraham also epitomizes for Derrida a moral attitude toward all others. Just as Abraham's desire for understanding is thwarted from the outset in the Genesis story, every subject must approach others in absurdity; epistemological desire goes out to the other but cannot recapture the other for the same. Therefore, in Derrida's terms, only because there is a secret, the other becomes Other for the I—upper-case, elevated, as a god. The radical alterity of subjects is guaranteed, because the Other persists as a secret, the secret of secret, so secret its secret essence is unknown even to its bearer. In Derrida's treatment, Abraham is the archetypical moral person, because his predicament is emblematic of all ethical relations: Abraham cannot know god's reasons for asking the absurd of him, just as every moral agent cannot know the other,

---

1 Jacques Derrida, *The Gift of Death*, David Wills, trans. (Chicago: University of Chicago Press, 1995).

but faces the other as Other, as god.[1] The god of Abraham is a secretive deity who keeps his reasons to himself when demanding the most radical sacrifice from Abraham. Abraham has no reason in this case, but keeps the secret from Sarah and Isaac.

---

1 Ibid., 57.

CHAPTER SEVEN. EVIL IN THE REASONS OF STATES

   Friedrich Nietzsche argues that strong, healthy natures can afford to forgive even great affronts from their enemies. The weak, on the other hand, feel every little slight and are humiliated by every threatening glance. They retaliate immediately over the slightest injury if means of retaliation present themselves; otherwise they seethe and fester with resentment awaiting an opportunity for revenge. For Nietzsche these distinctions hold true for individuals as well as states:

   As the power and self-confidence of a community increase, the penal law always becomes more moderate; every weakening or imperiling of the former brings with it a restoration of the harsher forms of the latter. The "creditor" always becomes more humane to the extent that he has grown richer; finally how much injury he can endure without suffering becomes the actual *measure* of his wealth. It is not unthinkable that a society might attain such a *consciousness of power* that it could allow itself the noblest luxury possible to it—letting those who harm it go unpunished. "What are my parasites to me?" it might say. "May they live and prosper; I am strong enough for that!"[1] Nietzsche

---

1 Friedrich Nietzsche, *On the Genealogy of Morals*, Walter Kaufmann, R. J. Hollingdale, tr. (New York: Random House, 1989), Essay II, Section 10, 72.

defines unhealthy natures as reactive, acting *in response* to perceived threats or injuries, and riddled with *ressentiment*, whereas
healthy natures are active, self-determining, shaping their forms
according to an internal aesthetic and their destinies according
to values they esteem.

Nietzsche's theory that violence and cruelty are functions
of a weak nature of low self-esteem is echoed throughout the
current favored social scientific theories on aggressive behaviors. Roy Baumeister is a social psychologist whose scholarly
research into the sorts of people who tend to commit cruel acts
takes a different view. In his *Evil: Inside Human Violence and Cruelty*
and other works, Baumeister disputes the current popular hypothesis (that low self-esteem motivates violence and cruelty).
Baumeister's research has convinced him that people who react
with aggression and cruelty largely hold themselves in high self-
esteem but perceive their high value is being questioned or their
superiority threatened.[1]

Whatever theory one follows, one fact seems certain: violence occurs largely because a perpetrator feels justified in doing
so. This explains why perpetrators rarely refer to their acts as
"evil" whereas victims use the term readily. Violence occurs as
a function of the *agent*'s disposition toward the world and thus
comes to be named by the agent as perhaps regrettable but always justifiable, but almost never as evil. People act cruelly because they feel individually threatened or affronted; states too
can perform acts that they would normally name evil in others, if
they feel vulnerable or disrespected by other groups or nations.

Anthropologists tell that the disposition toward violence
lurks as a latent possibility in every group's social rituals, embedded in their traditions and institutions, flaring forth in times
of crisis when people feel threatened, injured, or indignant.
People who are strong and not easily offended may be slower to
draw upon the timeless power of ritual to wreak vengeance on
their foes. Weak or strong, however, people are rarely willing to

---

1 Roy Baumeister, *Evil: Inside Human Violence and Cruelty* (? W. H. Freeman,
1999); *The Cultural Animal: Human Nature, Meaning, and Social Life* (Oxford,
Oxford University Press, 2005); Roy Baumeister, Brad J. Bushman, and
W. Keith Campbell, "Self-Esteem, Narcissism, and Aggression: Does
Violence Result from Low Self-Esteem or from Threatened Egoism?"
Current Directions in Psychological Science 9 (2000), 26-29.

admit that they do violence to others because they are simply disposed to do so. Rather—and this is the most baffling feature about violence—people most often do terrible things to others in full good conscience.

Individuals, groups and nations at war are quick to rally good "reasons" for their violences. Edward Said states:

> Every single empire in its official discourse has said that it is not like all the others, that its circumstances are special, that it has a mission to enlighten, civilize, bring to order and democracy, and that it uses force only as a last resort.[1]

From Hitler to Stalin, Pol Pot to Osama Bin Ladin, George W. Bush to Ariel Sharon, the official rhetoric called upon to sanctify state violences (whether internal restrictions of freedom to demonized minorities, or external violences to global neighbors encoded in foreign policies) generally calls upon the loftiest of ideals, as justification for their violence. History's worst violences tended to be framed in terms of a utopian ideal, a master-plan for some "new world order" that promises the finest results for humankind. From ancient Athens to Rome, from the various European empires across the globe to the Nazi reconstruction of Europe, to the modern United States, despite the vast time span and distances separating those imperial projects, states have learned little along the road of history about getting along with their neighbors. As Said remarks, the real irony is that the violences have always been, and continue to be, carried out in the name of all that is deemed good in those societies—order, national security, civilization, enlightenment, freedom, and democracy.

Since the earliest days of politics in the first city-states, people have been leery about trusting the fine speeches of politicians. Thus, it comes as little surprise to most of us when we learn that a president or a prime minister has done something we might name "evil." Somehow, we expect higher moral behavior from the ordinary citizen, uncorrupted by the burden of state responsibilities and the "harsh realities of power," than

---

1 Edward Said, "A window on the world" in *The Guardian*, August 2, 2003.

we expect from our politicians and demagogues. Thus we are prepared to understand political mistakes and huge bloopers that leave masses of foreigners dead in their sands, but we find ourselves entirely baffled when citizens like ourselves go badly astray. For all the unanswered questions about the Holocaust, the real mystery of that tragedy for many scholars remains: how did the ordinary German citizen get behind such a monstrous plan? What motivated Hitler's youth to rush to enlist for his military? How did so many "ordinary men" (to echo Christopher Browning's famed account of the German Reserve Police Battalion 101[1]), from middle-aged family men of the working class to professional soldiers like Adolf Eichmann, take up the twisted racist cause and enact the mass murders that effected Hitler's "Final Solution?"

The question of citizen complicity in mass murder maintains its impenetrable character across time and cultural terrain. However did ordinary citizens in Rwanda come to turn their machete blades upon the neighbors with whom, for centuries, they had shared small villages, their lives interwoven socially, economically, and politically (under tribally-alternating chiefdoms)? Again, more recently: how is it that those fresh-faced American G.I.s rushed excitedly to deliver democracy and freedom to the victims of Sadam Hussein's cruel rule, when the deliverance took the ironic form of a "Shock and Awe" blitzkrieg targeting heavily-populated urban areas that, in a matter of hours, "rescued" *by extermination* tens of thousands of innocent civilians. Perhaps most ironically, the civilian and military supporters of that campaign continue to hold to their ideological guns, despite the unprecedented global outcry that preceded that campaign, despite the fact that the campaign composes a breach of international law that alienated many US friends and allies, and despite the ensuing chaos that has unequivocally proven once again what logic, the military, and the political scientific community already predicted: that democracy imposed on a people violently is just another form of tyranny.

It seems clear that we can add to Said's pessimistic statement the corollary that it is not simply the leaders of empires

---

1 Christopher R. Browning, *Ordinary Men: Reserve Police Battalion 101 and the Final Solution in Poland*, New York: HarperCollins, 1992.

that are comfortable with the use of extreme force to achieve their "special missions" and their "new world orders," but ordinary people within those empires by and large accept readily and in good conscience their leader's facile justifications for atrocities against demonized others, both inside and external to their homeland. Ordinary people seem all too comfortable to condone and participate in their leader's violent projects, to take up the sword to slaughter a neighbor when a war cry is sounded on the home soil. Though people in general give lip service to global peace and justice, we are ever little more than a national anthem, a flag-waving, or a pledge of allegiance away from the next bloodbath of the next enemy. It is difficult to argue with the vast majority of anthropologists of violence who claim that all people are fundamentally violence-prone. We need all be concerned, as Browning is, about the degree to which the criminally aggressive policies of our political regimes permeate everyday existence.[1]

As a result of the apparent and troubling ubiquity of violence in the world, a good many people, whether religious believers or not, are ready to accept the fundamentally religious explanation for the violence they perceive: that something commonly named "evil" abounds. People can, and do, mean very different things when they employ the term "evil," but there is little doubt that the notion of evil proves highly functional for explaining the incidence of extreme violence and cruelty in the world. There is also very little doubt that a worldview that includes a notion of evil can easily be put to work to provide a convenient excuse for a great many bad actions that would, otherwise, be unjustifiable.

Many people believe that evil exists. It is equally the case that few people would be prepared to locate the site of the emergence of that evil at their own home-site of existence, within their own existential spaces—in the behavior codes of *their* family, in the social conventions of *their* cultural group, in the beliefs of *their* religious group, or in the policies of *their* nation. Something deep within each one of us seems to dictate that the homespaces where *our* identities are seated, and the practices and loyalties whereby *our* characters are constructed, remain persistently sacred and beyond moral question, whereas the

---

1 Ibid., xix.

homespaces of others are readily suspect. For the mainstream of people, evil remains a phenomenon *out there* inhabiting strange lifeworlds, emanating from alien others and motivating foreign people's behaviors.

To understand how moral complacency attends people in the darkest of their historical moments, predisposing them to seek violent, rather than peaceful, solutions to the problems that arise to challenge them, the scholar must appreciate how people's interpretations of world events are intimately entangled with their social, religious, and philosophical preconceptions and how these preconceptions themselves found moral ideals and values and systems of virtues. The very ideas that people hold sacred and trust to guide them in their daily actions, to aid them in making sound judgments and morally viable decisions as they go about their projects in the world may prone "good" people toward conscience-free violence. If we are to understand how "evil" happens and how it comes to be justified on the home front of its perpetration, we must strive to comprehend and chart the historical frameworks within which people think and act, and to understand the truth assumptions that give rise to a people's perceptions of good and evil, and discover whether, and, if so, where and to what extent, evil seeps through, or is indeed embedded in, the good intentions and lofty ideals that form the horizons of a people's lifeworld.

1. Civilization and Evil

The vast majority of violence research that has been carried out up until now approaches violence as anomalous, as a breakdown in the norm of healthy, cooperative relations among human communities. The underlying assumption is that, unless something goes terribly wrong, peace will reign supreme under the moral dictates encoded in the traditions we name "civilization." However, if we are willing to risk this comforting assumption and look seriously at the history of the human species, we ought rather come to the opposite conclusion. Human beings killed their fellows from the opening moments of human time, but they began the mass slaughter of their neighbors only

with the advent of *civitas*—the state.[1] With the rise of the ordered community, the sanctified concept of a territorial home,
a fatherland, was carved out. There must exist a strong sense of
a righteous and sacred home territory to bring the enemy alien
into conceptual clarity. Sacred home-sites of identity are established through a religious mechanism that projects internal evils
onto alien presences within or outside of the home group. With
the gesture of demonization of the alien, the enemy is brought to
birth. Also brought to birth in this process are the categories of
sacred and profane, good and evil.

With the birth of the state, "civilization" is born and so is
war. The aggressive impulses of the populace that cause unrest
within the community can be redirected, through fervent rituals
of nationalism, onto the entire world alien to the sacred fatherland. We see the demonization mechanism quite clearly in the
language of the first empire-builders of the West, the ancient
Greeks, who carved the entire world into two vast categories
of people—the Hellenes and everybody else, named loosely *bar-
baroi*, an alliterative mimicry of foreigners' "barbaric" speech
which sounded to the Greeks like stuttering or the barking of
an animal.

We also see, in the example of ancient Greece, the birth of
another phenomenon, which demonstrates how popular ideas of
good and evil come to evolve over the course of historico-socio-
economic transformations. The Greek term that was employed
to speak of the ancient race of kings and princes was *aristoi* (the
English term "aristocracy" comes from *aristos*—noble, kingly—
and *kratein*—to rule). The varied uses and extensions of this
term verify Heidegger's statement that "language is the house of
Being." They also confirm that the power nodes of this society,
as in any society, held control both *of* and *through* language. *Aristoi* is connected to the terms *aristos* (good, noble) and *arēte* (the
manly virtues of noble men). The language confirms the cultural
"truth" that only the princely class was excellent and worthy of
rule in Greek city-states.

This class prejudice, brought to reification in language,
implies so much more than is readily apparent. Since for the

---

1 Eli Sagan, *The Dawn of Tyranny The Origins of Individualism, Political
Oppression, and the State* (New York: Knopf, 1985).

Greeks, being is divinely-empowered and hierarchically ordered from the least powerful and good to the best, the wise and noble gods direct the human adventure, bringing to birth the *right* kind of sons in the *right* kind of families to rule over the lesser populations, the *hoi polloi* or "the many" (a term still employed to speak of the lowly and vulgar masses). These common folk were understood to suffer not so much from the evil of malevolence as from the evil of ignorance. After all, reason is what human souls share with the gods and the "many" are the humans farthest removed from the gods. How much could a simple peasant know in his degraded state of being, how well educated might he become, how much time could he devote to philosophy, politics, and the fluctuating realities of the law courts and war councils, when relegated every day to the field, struggling close to the cusp of existence, bound in the constant battle with hunger, disease, and death?

The aristocratic prejudice—that birth determines worth—is confirmed throughout the writings of the early Greek philosophers. In the *Republic*, Plato plans a city in *logos* that ensures that only the right kinds of people will emerge to rule. The right kind of people for rule are those born with the right qualities (philosophers and guardians). The powerful are relieved from menial labors. Their bodily needs are fulfilled by the labor of the less worthy citizens, that they may concentrate their superior intellect and passion on the rigorous work of state rule. A fiction, the "myth of the metals," ensures that the low-born stay in their place and that the well-born remain in control. However, in admitting the founding myth as a "noble lie" and allowing the rulers discretionary power over class borderlines, Plato is also admitting that the gods can be wrong, that noble birth does not ensure nobleness of character, especially where education has not done its proper work. As much as Plato, as an aristocrat, is predisposed against democracy *per se*, he shows in the *Republic* that he holds good character to be of greater importance than good birth. What is most crucial to the sound state is that leadership remain in the hands of those who are *aristoi* in character, the noble-minded who have superior ethical vision, who have overcome base materialist urges and do not suffer from the lust for power. The leader must be he—or she!—who loves not the goods craved in Athens (money, possessions, honors, and power). Indeed she distinguishes herself for fitness to rule by her lack of interest in monetary affairs and the ownership of valuable possessions, by her disdain for the handling of money, and by her reluctance for the position of leadership.

Ironically, despite softening the boundaries between the *aristoi* and *hoi polloi* in the *Republic*'s city in *logos*, Plato confirms the features of *arete* (masculine aristocratic virtues) as the distinguishing qualities for leadership. In confirming aristocratic virtues, Plato reconfirms the rightness of the tradition of power relations in Athens before democracy opened the ranks of power to the wealthy common merchants. Who but the wealthy can afford to care little for possessions? Who but the wealthy are in a position to develop a healthy distain for the handling of money? Who but the wealthy can develop the liberality of spirit crucial to guardian barracks life? Who but the wealthy can afford the free time to learn to appreciate the goods of the mind over the goods of the body? Who but those of privilege will benevolently shepherd the common flock instead of fleece them for personal profit?

Notions of evil are evolving during this period and breaking through the linguistic and social barriers that govern the popular worldview of Athenians. *Aristos* is exploding the barriers of noble birth and demanding demonstration in worldly acts. One obvious signal of this change is Socrates' quest for right definitions. Socrates insists that the terms used in everyday conversation fit the social realities to which people attach them. Socrates insists that the gap be closed between the lofty words (*logoi*) attached to noble persons (*aristos*) and the often baser deeds (*ergoi*) being performed in the cities and on the battlefields.

Socrates' earliest linguistic challenges to his Athenian fellows in his questions *What is it?* and *How do you say it?* highlight that their words must be linked to their deeds—that goodness *is* as goodness *does*. The princely caste measure their moral superiority by unbroken birth-lines descending from heroes and gods. The Olympian divines smile down on their chosen offspring and bring them good fortune in their adventures and good winds in their wars, often fighting alongside them in their battles to ensure their worldly successes. By insisting that the speaker pay close attention to the words that she employs to speak about things, Socrates highlights that virtues must have their demonstration in generous and noble works. To know the good is to do the good, and to do the good is to be named rightly the good. Thus the designation of *aristos* belongs to those who behave noble-mindedly toward others, who effect no harm in their daily deeds, and who cultivate their souls to a state of righteousness, rather than those who lay claim to noble bloodlines.

Socrates insists the noble act well, but he remains ambiguous on the question of the whether low-born are capable of noble character. Socrates tells Theaetetus that philosophers care nothing for birth and know nothing about the familial lineages of their citizen fellows; on the other hand, Socrates has already shown in conversation with Theodoras that he knows intimately the details of Theaetetus' lineage.[1] He affirms his family's long lineage from the mythical hero Daedalus and claims special relations to the gods Apollo and Zeus.[2] And though Socrates states the philosopher pays no attention to ancestry, he often demonstrates that he knows in great detail the intimate particulars of his interlocutors' birth line.[3]

While words and concepts are being held to more and more exacting scrutiny, notions of good and evil are evolving too, during Socrates and Plato's lifetime. As the old well-born families fall from the exclusive socio-political superiority they long enjoyed and rich merchant classes push into the forefront of power in the new Athenian democracy, the appellations (*aristoi*) that had set apart the old families as best people and fittest rulers (*aristoi*) lose their social anchors. Good and evil demand redefinition. Slowly philosophical challenges and the new political actualities affect popular attitudes about what realities constitute good and evil. Moral terms begin to be used to describe the actions and behaviors of individuals, rather than to identity social class.

2. The Uses of Evil

The language of evil is very old, compelling, and seductive,

---

1 Plato, *Theaetetus*
2 Connection with Daedalus at Euthyph. 11b; Socrates is a son of Apollo (Apol. 21b) and follows in the train of Zeus (Phaedr. 250b)
3 Theaet. 144c contra 173d.

steeped in moralistic overtones and entrenched in violent ritual tradition, which facts explain its frequent resurfacing in diverse historical eras at times of social and political crisis. Talk of evil tends to have a gripping effect on audiences. The language of evil crops up regularly across the historico-political landscape in the least likely of times and places, because it very effectively serves important pragmatic functions in the life of a person, a people, and a state.

First, the mythology of evil serves important political functions. In *Genealogy of Morals*, Friedrich Nietzsche demonstrates that people use the terms "good" and "evil" to distinguish themselves from others. Powerful, healthy (hyper-masculine, military) cultures value noble birth, strength, bravery, liberality of spirit, honesty, and loyalty. A culture that is disempowered will use "good" to affirm their characteristics but their efforts will culminate in an inverted morality, a reactive morality born of resentment for those in power.[1] Starkly moralizing worldviews affirm the rightness of the status quo of power relations by demonizing outsiders to the group. For the weak in society, hyper-moralities make people feel better about who they are, and about their disadvantaged status. The multi-dimensional functionality of moralizing worldviews explains their prolonged existence long after people's social relations and historical circumstances have shifted course.

People don't question the mythology of evil that counsels projects of vengeance because the mythical worldview not only serves political functions for the powerful, but serves crucial existential needs in the lives of the least privileged of citizens as well. The cognitive filtering that heightens the subject's experience of the enemy as exaggeratedly potent and malevolent has a secondary and important existential effect: it amplifies the sense of victim identity as innocent and vulnerable. Because so many people in any political system are victims of that system, the language of evil resonates fiercely with their experience of the world.

However tragic and hopeless people's existences, whatever adversities and privations they suffer, people take great comfort

[1] Ibid.

in a worldview where everything is strictly ordered and makes sense. The grand cosmic struggle between good and evil trivializes people's mundane concerns like grueling labor, poverty, disease, and the hungry bellies and untimely deaths of their children. Though things may look dark, the mythology of good and evil places the god at the helm of earthly events and guarantees that all will be well in the final accounting. The god repays the suffering of worldly misfortune in a transcendental gift system; the meek shall inherit the earth in an afterlife that rewards their docile obedience.

The myth of evil serves other existential needs peculiar to modern democratic society. The notion of evil and the ritual of the purging of evil provides enemies we can despise *together*, thereby forging from the diversity that composes modern societies the "common mental world" that is essential to people's mental health.[1] Moreover, because evil is a morally significant experience, the event of its destruction supplies an episode of ecstatic release from the numbing mediocrity of consumer society, a release that is ecstatic, thrilling, freeing.[2]

Evil comes to appearance exaggerated by fear and loathing within a victim worldview where definitions are categorical and identities are ordered and distinct. Discourses of evil give moral texture to human lives, an illusion of meaning to life events, allowing for stark, clear, morally-significant identity boundaries, and clarifying the work of the god's faithful. Evil myths achieve these important goals in human lives by locating those beings or forces that do not hold rank in the god's holy army, those who transgress the moral boundaries of polite human society, creeping in from some moral netherworld.

The myth of evil posits that the world makes sense; bad things happen because evil is. By radically polarizing contested identities, the myth of evil appears to give meaning to tragedy and chaos. It furnishes a sense of a complete explanation; there is no need, indeed no sense, in searching any further for failures in oneself or in the system at large. It is as though, in naming someone or

---

1 See note 6.
2 Aristotle tells that "a certain pleasure [*tina hedonen*], which derives from the hope of punishing [*timoresasthai*], accompanies every experience of anger" (*Rhetoric* 1378b1-2).

something evil, we place it across a border, a safe and comforting boundary. Beyond that limit, a dark and monstrous reality lurks, incomprehensible to human minds. By tossing all that we do not understand on the far side of that border, our identity remains pure and pristine. No matter whom we may harm in the world, we are reasonable, rational, moral, and more human because others are evil monsters. But the meaningfulness is simply illusion. The term evil adds nothing to our understanding of people or events. In fact, naming others evil forbids their investigation.

People are quick to see evil in things because at times very bad things happen that seem to defy explanation. It is easy to explain the worst crimes in history by attributing them to monsters. But Christopher Browning demonstrates that "ordinary men" populated the ranks of the crack killing battalions of the Third Reich. Ordinary mothers in Poland and Lithuania brought picnic lunches and held their children up to witness the mass executions of their Jewish neighbors. In Rwanda, ordinary Hutu mothers were reported to turn in their husbands and half-Tutsi children for execution, in response to the Hutu extremist propaganda (adapted from the colonial mythology) that Tutsi were foreign "cockroaches" feeding off genuine African peoples.[1]

Extreme terms and rigid mythologies can comfort the downtrodden in a world that is harsh and violence-ridden, but the sad truth is that the bad things people call "evil" are not something special and rare. They are frightfully common—ordinary, banal. "Evils" come to us in many forms that we can do little to circumvent: floods and earthquakes, ageing, disease and death. And evil comes to us in forms that should make us want to change the world: hunger, ignorance, homelessness, epidemic, wars and oppression.

Discourses of evil and their attendant mythologies do not help in the healing of victims; they do not help us to understand *why* bad things happen, nor do they clarify *how* to avoid them in the future. Rational deliberation of what constitutes "due measure" in every case restores the balance of justice that lets every-

---

1 Hutu adapted aspects of the divide-and-conquer politics of the colonials that had propagandized the notion of distinct tribal identity and the "Hamitic hypothesis" that rendered Tutsis "Arabic intruders" from the northeast.

one move forward from tragedies. When ethical challenges and socio-political difficulties are the focus, people are prompted to work together to reach solutions beneficial to all, to protect future victims from harm, to heal those who have been harmed, and to improve the human condition for all.

As long as we employ the imagery of evil in talking about human tragedies, we free ourselves from responsibility for seeking just remedies for bad things. When we see things and people as evil, our responses become extreme. Then we risk legitimating the use of violent methods that we would readily name evil in others. Since the myth of evil serves no valuable explanatory purposes and does not enhance moral response but actually frustrates justice and triggers cycles of violent response, I am recommending that, once and for all, we put to rest these extremist terms of discussion in the graveyard of outdated and dangerous relics that belong to a mythical world.

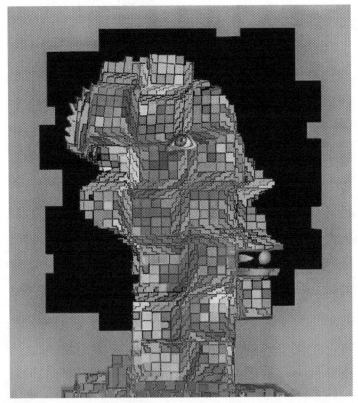

CHAPTER EIGHT. SEE NO EVIL. DO NO EVIL

People conceive of evil in a variety of ways. In this work, Martin Camarata and I have imaged and articulated some of those many ways. We have intimated too by our images and musings the ways in which these conceptualizations can change the conceivers, orienting them in the direction of those very attitudes and behaviors that they would readily deem "evil" in others. We have seen that despite the plethora of variation in individual conceptualizations of evil, one thing that the conceivers quasi-universally share in common is the tendency to reserve the term "evil" for the things that *other people* do. It is easy for most people to see where *others* go wrong and easy too to imagine malice and cruel delight as playing a pivotal role in *other people's* actions, but almost universally, people see their own misdeeds, however harmful, as merely innocent accidents or miscalculations, unfortunate collateral damage necessarily sacrificed to some greater good or cause, or sound reasoning in matters of moral necessity demanding the control and containment of dangerous others. It is part and parcel of the phenomenality of evil that it comes to appearance as "out there" in other people's reality, to be tried "objectively" by judicious observers. Rarely, if ever, do evil phenomena emanate from subjective self-assessment; evil is always at a distance from the subject, even when the cruel fallout bleeds over into their existential space.

In fact the one-sidedness that is a fundamental aspect of the phenomenon of evil helps to illuminate the existential purpose being served by the phenomenon: its very seeing distances the subject from what she morally rejects, closing off the frightening possibility that she too might be capable of heinous misdeeds. It is not that the phenomenon of evil *falsely* appears as "objective," since the question of truth or falsity is always already an inappropriate question for the phenomenologist. Phenomenology attempts to naively record things as they truly appear to subjects, and since we have no recourse to some pure account of reality, untainted by the subject's perception, there is no way to compare phenomena *as they appear* to some original event that is more real or true. In short, the fact that evil *as a phenomenon* comes into view as an aspect of reality "out there" equates to stating that the phenomenon is truly and really *experienced as* "out there" in somebody else's domain of action. One cannot challenge the veracity of this experience as real for the perceiver. Edmund Husserl would go farther and state that no one, not even the supposedly objective scientist, can challenge the veracity of phenomena, because the scientist enjoys no pure access to "things in themselves" unmediated by perception.

The fact that evil comes to appearance as causally distanced from the subject tells more about the subject, than the object of that experience: it reveals that subjects rarely have the ability or inclination to turn the critical judgmental eye upon themselves. This inability amounts to a moral blindness right at the site of moral judgment. And it explains why subjects rarely suffer from the cognitive dissonance that we might reasonably expect them to suffer when aspects of their own thoughts and behaviors fit their own definitions of evil.

A second aspect of the phenomenon of evil that is very revealing of the subject is the fact that the other person's evil not only comes clearly into view at this safe existential distance, but it tends to come into view already distilled and pronounced. The experience of evil is an emotionally-charged experience that frames phenomena in an extreme way, by comparison with ordinary everyday occurrences. Evil things come to appearance as always already heightened in their phenomenality. This heightening is paradoxical in nature, because it amounts to having an illuminated quality while simultaneously appearing darkened. That is to say that evil phenomena come to appear as exaggerated in potency and malevolence. Though, to reaffirm the limitations imposed on the phenomenologist by the parameters of her investigation, we cannot ask the rule on the truth or falsity of this hyper-recognition, but we can compare how the same objects come to appearance very differently when the subject is in a different subjective state. Take for example, the child who is terrified by the huge, dark figure of a malevolent beast that emerges into his phenomenal awareness from out of his closet when the lights are turned out. The same child will experience this creature very differently when the light of day reveals his hockey shirt on a hanger at the closet door. The difference between these two experiences raises the question of the degree to which subjectivity itself, in its varying emotional states, is admixed in the experience of the other. It seems that this darker, more exaggerated seeing would occur primarily under the influence of fear, disgust, or dread.

The phenomenal paradoxes associated with the experience of evil raise a fruitful possibility for our serious consideration: that evil may not be, as it appears to be, "out there" in someone else's reality, but right here in human perceptions of the unknown, ready to disappear in the comforting light of greater awareness. Or the paradox may instead open onto a more frightening possibility: since every object is potentially a subject, perhaps every subject can be accurately described as capable of evil. And if everyone is potentially evil, then no one *kind of person* is uniquely captured by the epithet. That is, there exist no pure victims and no pure perpetrators. No victim, however deeply harmed by another, is an utterly passive being, awaiting degradation at another's hand, just as no perpetrator, however cruel and brutal his actions, lacks a core of potential goodness. Every person is a mixed bundle of possibilities. And when people come to harm, it is often as part of a dynamic that involves numerous parties. Evil, if it can be said to exist at all beyond the gap between monsters and hockey shirts, is best understood as a dance in which multiple persons engage, all with limited vision of their contribution to the escalation and destructiveness of the rave.

Therefore, we hope that this work on evil has offered the

reader a revelation about the phenomenon that recommends a postponement of her subjective adjudication of evil others. We hope that the broader perspective of this work has persuaded the reader to approach things and people with eyes wider open, to enable them to see that those whom we understand to morally fail us are not simply and purely evil, but rather, much the same as everyone else—complicated bundles of moral differences, sometimes triggered to act in bad judgment by fear, disgust, and dread. The very way we approach, see, and condemn these paradoxical others can contribute to their moral failure, even as the phenomenon of their evil can motivate our own evil response. It is safer, more accurate, and certainly more charitable to approach others in their radical difference, in the spirit condensed in my friend's characterization of her husband: "He's like a box of chocolates; you never know what you'll get!"

It is not that the people and things we don't understand are purely good any more than they are purely evil; it is that reality arises in the meeting ground that connects subjects, and so no subjective view of others is ever truly objective. Sometimes others give forth the syrupy essence that fills our souls with delight, releasing the warm, caramel feelings that make us glad to be alive alongside them—and sometimes our teeth meet their rocky reality in ways that break loose our fillings. But whatever our subjective experience of them, the universal feature that connects almost all perpetrators—the fact of their common victimization and suffering of violence in their tender years—should give us pause before we rush to judgments of evil. Maybe we are all just doing the best we can. Perhaps when people do evil to others, their choices are shaped and conditioned just as our phenomenal experiences are—by fear, disgust, and dread.

AFTERWORD

At about 10:15 in the morning of the 11ᵗʰ of April, 1987, Primo Levi, Jewish-Italian chemist and survivor of Auschwitz, threw himself down the stairwell of the old Turin house where he had been born. Like many survivors of phenomena most people would agree to exemplify "evil," Levi had learned in Auschwitz dark truths about human nature and the workings of human societies that would permanently alter his view of the world and cripple his potential for happiness. The most striking and most unbearable truth that Levi learned in the context of that paradigm among twentieth-century evils, which he analyzes at length in his *The Drowned and the Saved*, was the permeable border separating the identities of victims and perpetrators. Levi discovered in Auschwitz that survival in the face of evil requires ordinary human beings to slip across that definitive line and contribute to the brutality around them. The human soul, in its purest form, may be crystalline and wholesome, as Plato pictured it in the *Republic* (Rep. 10.611bc) but its purity is readily sullied on the downslide into hell. Levi learned this sad truth in Auschwitz, but he declares it a universal reality:

> [T]he harsher the oppression, the more widespread among the oppressed is the willingness. with all its in-finite nuances and motivations, to collaborate: terror,

ideological seduction, servile imitation of the victor, myopic desire for any power whatsoever, even though ridiculously circumscribed in space and time, cowardice, and finally lucid calculation aimed at eluding the imposed orders and order. All these motives, singly or combined, have come into play in the creation of [a] grey zone, whose components are bonded together by the wish to preserve and consolidate established privilege vis-à-vis those without privilege.[1]

Levi's revelation resonates with the thesis of Hannah Arendt's *Eichmann in Jerusalem*: evil is banal—ordinary and mundane. Levi's refusal of the Nazi death-camp survivor as somehow purified by his experience forces the reader to recognize the inadequacy of accepted understandings of the world and the human condition, grounded in clear and distinct definitions, sorted and ordered according to a polarized logic of good and evil. Levi holds up his account of Auschwitz as a mirror before us and forces us to peer deep into the universal "human" reality writ large in the Nazi death camp. In that mirror, we see that ordinary people can sidestep their consciences and do terrible things to get ahead among their fellows. Dehumanizing systems like National Socialism are more extreme than other systems, but all systems dehumanize. The distinction between them is not one of kind but only degree.

Levi contends that, though the Auschwitz lager was an especially cruel and degenerate system, the network of human relations that formed there constituted a typically "human" society, a microcosmic community that is, in fundamental respects, analogous to all human communities. Levi insists that systems shape people, compose their deepest reality and dictate their behaviors and responses to others. People quickly adopt the logic of their system and unthinkingly adjust their conduct to fit its policies and practices.

The camp demonstrated with frightening clarity the sociological fact that the desire to belong within a comprehensible world is so integrally necessary for human survival that even the most oppressed within the system will endorse the system

1 Primo Levi. *The Drowned and the Saved*. Roman Rosenthal, trans. (New York: Vintage Books, 1989), p. 43.

that oppresses them. Systems maintain order through ritual-ized observances that confirm a logic of domination, within pre-established networks of social status that rank and order the population according to system values, and assert strict patterns of political arrangements and economic exchange. All systems are to some degree coercive structures that effect social control through top-down monopolization of violence; strict rituals maintain the logic of the system and undermine nobler instincts, from the height to the depths of the social ladder.[1]

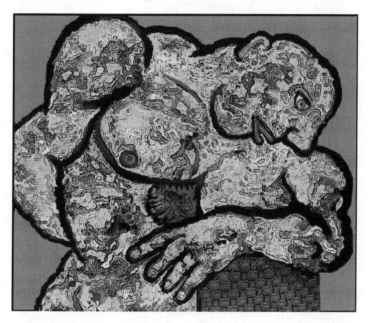

Levi understands the human need for simple categories and clear distinctions to make sense of the ambiguities and confu-sions of life, and he believes Holocaust survivors and historians rethink the Lager experience in the light of this human need. They sort the people in this human story into "good guys" and "bad guys" so their worlds can feel safe. But no clear distinctions allow a neat sorting between the "the [morally] drowned" from "the [morally] saved."

Anyone who today reads (or writes) the history of

1 Ibid. p. 39-40.

the Lager reveals the tendency, indeed the need, to separate evil from good, to be able to take sides, to emulate
Christ's gesture on Judgment Day: here the righteous,
over there the reprobates.[1]

The distinctions between perpetrators and victims within a
system are not so clear as we would have them; most sociological
reality falls into the "grey zone." Perpetrators are often victims of
the system; victims readily turn perpetrator when their morals
bump up against the urgent necessity to survive.

The National Socialist regime was a system crueler and more
dehumanizing than most. The harsher the system, asserts Levi,
the more pervasive among the oppressed is the readiness to col-
laborate with its cruel practices (Levi, 1989, 43). The lager, tells
Levi, was a system entirely typical, not aberrant or anomalous.
Systems are always, by nature, violent. They are always, at least
to some degree, coercive hierarchies that mold their members
in their image. All communities, to greater or lesser degrees, in
their very struggle to exist, pit individual against individual. The
powerful look to maintain their power by forming powerful alli-
ances. The oppressed look for relief from their abjection by claw-
ing their way to the top of others. The lagers demonstrate, in mi-
crocosm, that relief from oppression within systems comes only
through compliance with the system, by taking up the injustices
of the system and embracing them as one's own.

Systems "degrade the people within them, make them resemble itself, and this all the more when they are available, blank,
and lacking a political or moral armature."[2] Levi's warning serves
as a fitting introduction to a book on evil. But, if he is correct
in his claim that all systems are analogous in structure, then it
would seem to be imperative that our systems develop the "moral armature" that Levi recommends as their saving grace.

However, I would suggest that a moral armature is always
already in place in every social structure, else it would not be
an ordered structure. The reasons explaining the ranking and
ordering at play in the state—whether those reasons are political, historical, economic, or social—are always already morally

1 Ibid. p. 37.
2 Levi, *The Drowned and the Saved* (New York: Random House, 1989), 40.

significant justifications for the inequalities that exist. Indeed it is not so much that the moral armature is missing as that the system arrives complete with unassailable moral armature; the moral armature is often the problem and not the solution to evil. Even National Socialism had a moral armature; it worshipped courage, genetic purity, disciplined obedience, unquestioning loyalty. Moreover, it promised redemption to a people beaten down and shamed by the humiliating terms of their losses from the First World War. That is the thing about ideology: it always has moral significance for its holders.

BIBLIOGRAPHY

Alvis, John. *Divine Purpose and Heroic Response in Homer and Virgil.* Lanham, MD. Rowman & Littlefield. 1995.

Arendt, Hannah. *The Human Condition.* Chicago. University of Chicago Press. 1958.

———. *The Life of the Mind.* New York. Harcourt, Brace & Co. 1971.

———. *On Revolution.* New York. Penguin. 1973.

———. *On Violence.* New York. Harcourt, Brace & Co. 1970.

Baker, S.W. "The Races of the Nile Basin" in *Transactions of the Ethnological Society of London,* N.S.V. 1867.

Bartos, Otomar, and Paul Weir. *Using Conflict Theory.* Cambridge. Cambridge University Press. 2002.

Bataille, Georges. "Reflections on the Executioner and the Victim." *Yale French Studies. Literature and the Ethical Question.* Number 79. Claire Nouvet, ed. New Haven. Yale University Press. 1991, 15-19.

Baumeister, Roy F. *Evil: Inside Human Violence and Cruelty.* New York. Freeman & Co. 1997.

Browning, Christopher R. *Ordinary Men: Reserve Police Battalion 101 and the Final Solution in Poland.* New York. Harper Perennial. 1998.

Burkert, Walter. *Structure and History in Greek Myth and Ritual.* Berkeley. University of California Press. 1979.

———. *Homo Necans: An Anthropology of Ancient Greek Sacrificial Ritual and Myth.* Peter Bing, trans. Berkeley. University of California Press. 1983.

———. *Creation of the Sacred: Tracks of Biology in Early Religions.* Cambridge, Mass.: Harvard University Press. 1996.

Cambridge Companion to Plato. Richard Kraut, ed. Cambridge University Press. 1992.

Caputo, A., et al. "Understanding and Experiences of Cruelty: An Exploratory Report." *The Journal of Social Psychology.* 140(5), 649-660.

Collins, Randall. *Four Sociological Traditions: Selected Readings.* Oxford. Oxford University Press. 1994.

Cropsey, Joseph. *Plato's World: Man's Place in the Cosmos.* University of Chicago Press. 1995.

Cross, R.C. and A.D.Woosley. "Knowledge, Belief and the Forms." *Plato: A Collection of Critical Essays.* Gregory Vlastos, ed. Anchor Books. Garden City, NY. 1971.

Dallmayr, Fred. *The Other Heidegger.* Ithaca. Cornell University Press. 1993.

Dawkins, Richard. *The Selfish Gene.* Oxford. Oxford University Press. 1976.

Delaney, Carol. *Abraham on Trial.* Princeton. Princeton University Press. 2000.

Derrida, Jacques. *"Structure, Sign and Play in the Discourse of the Human Sciences."* *Critical Theory Since 1965.* H. Adams and L. Searle, eds. Gainesville, Florida.: Florida State University Press. 1986. 83-94.

———. *The Gift of Death*, David Wills, trans. Chicago. University of Chicago Press. 1995.

Diamond, Jared. *Guns, Germs and Steel.* New York. W. W. Norton. 2005.

Dodds, E.R. "Plato and the Irrational Soul." *Plato II.* G. Vlastos, ed. Doubleday. Garden City, N.Y. 1971.

Dorter, Kenneth. "The Phaedo's Final Argument." *New Essays on Plato and the PreSocratics.* R.A.Shiner. J.King-Farlow, eds. Canadian Association for Publishing in Philosophy. Guelph, Ontario. 1976.

Dostoevsky, Fyodor. *The Brothers Karamazov.* New York. Barnes and Noble Books. 1995.

Evans-Pritchard, E.E. *Theories of Primitive Religion.* London. Oxford University Press. 1965.

Freeman, W.H. *The Cultural Animal: Human Nature, Meaning, and Social Life.* Oxford. Oxford University Press. 2005.

Girard, René. *Violence and the Sacred.* Patrick Gregory, trans. Baltimore. Johns Hopkins University Press. 1979.

Griswold, Charles L., Jr. *Self-Knowledge in Plato's* Phaedrus. Pennsylvania State University Press. University Park, Pennsylvania. 1986.

Grossman, David. *On Killing: The Psychological Cost of Learning to Kill in War and*

Society. New York. Little, Brown & Co. 1995.

Gulley, Norman. *Plato's Theory of Knowledge.* Methuen. London. 1962.

Guthrie, W.K.C. "Plato's Views on the Nature of the Soul." *Plato II.* G.Vlastos, ed. Doubleday. Garden City, N.Y. 1971.

Hamblet, Wendy. *Savage Constructions: The Myth of African Savagery* Lanham, MD. Lexington Books. 2008.

Heidegger, Martin. *An Introduction to Metaphysics.* Ralph Mannheim, trans. New Haven. Yale University Press,. 1959.

Hyland, Drew A.. *Finitude and Transcendence in the Platonic Dialogues.* State University of New York Press. 1995.

James, William. *Varieties of Religious Experience.* New York. Modern Library. 1994.

Kierkegaard, Søren. *Fear and Trembling.* London. Oxford University Press. 1939.

Kirk, G.S., and J. E. Raven, *The Presocratic Philosophers.* London. Cambridge University Press. 1957.

Koenigsberg, Richard. *Hitler's Ideology: A Study in Psychoanalytic Sociology.* New York. Library of Social Science. 1975.

Lenski, Gerhard E. *Power and Privilege: A Theory of Social Stratification.* New York. McGraw-Hill. 1966.

Levi, Primo. *The Drowned and the Saved.* Raymond Rosenthal, trans. New York: Vintage Books. 1989.

Levinas, Emmanuel. *Totality and Infinity: An Essay on Exteriority.* Alfonso Lingis, trans. Pittsburgh. Duquesne University Press. 1969.

————. *Collected Philosophical Papers*, Alfonso Lingis, trans. Dordrecht. Kluwer Academic Publishers, 1986.

————. *Nine Talmudic Readings.* Annette Aronowicz, trans. Bloomington. Indiana University Press. 1990.

————. "The Trace of the Other." *Deconstruction in Context.* Mark Taylor, ed. Chicago. University Of Chicago Press. 1986.

Lévy-Bruhl, Lucien. *Primitive Mentality.* Lilian A. Claire, trans. London. Allen & Unwin, and New York. MacMillan. 1923.

————. *The Notebooks on Primitive Mentality.* Peter Rivière, trans. New York. Harper & Row. 1975.

Lorenz, Konrad. *On Aggression.* Marjorie Kerr Wilson, trans. New York. Harcourt, Brace and World. 1966.

McGowan, John. *Hannah Arendt.* Minneapolis. University of Minnesota Press. 1998.

Mills, Linda G. *Violent Partners.* New York. Basic Books. 2008.

Nehamas, Alexandre. *The Art of Living*. University of California Press. Berkeley. 1998.

Nietzsche, Friedrich. *The Birth of Tragedy*. Walter Kaufmann, trans. New York. Vintage Books. 1967.

———. *On the Genealogy of Morals*. Walter Kaufmann, trans. New York. Vintage Books, 1989.

———. *Ecce Homo*. Walter Kaufmann, trans. New York. Vintage Books. 1989.

———. *Thus Spoke* Zarathustra, Manuel Komroff, trans. New York. Tudor. 1889.

Nussbaum, Martha C. *The Fragility of Goodness*. Cambridge. Cambridge University Press. 1986.

Pinker, Steven. *The Blank Slate*. Camrbidge. Harvard University Press. 2003.

Plato: *The Collected Dialogues*. Edith Hamilton. Huntington Cairns, eds. Princeton University Press. 1961.

Radin, Paul. *Primitive Religion*. New York. Dover. 1937.

Ritter, C. *The Essence of Plato's Philosophy*. London. Allen & Unwin. 1933.

Robinson, T.M.. *Plato's Psychology*. University of Toronto Press. Toronto. 1970.

Rubinoff, Lionel. *The Pornography of Power*. New York. Ballantine Books,. 1969.

Russell, Jeffrey B. *The Devil*. Ithaca, N.Y. Cornell University Press. 1977.

Sallis, John. *Being and Logos*. Indiana University Press. Bloomington. 1996.

Said, Edward. "A Window on the World" in *The Guardian*, August 2, 2003.

Sagan, Eli. *The Dawn of Tyranny The Origins of Individualism, Political Oppression, and the State*. New York. Knopf. 1985.

Sapolsky, Robert. "Pseudokinship and the Real War." *San Francisco Chronicle*. March 2, 2003, D3.

Seligman, Paul. *The Self as Principle of Order*. (unpublished).

Skemp, J.B. *The Theory of Motion in Plato's Later Dialogues*. Cambridge University Press. Cambridge. 1942.

Stoyanov, Yuri. *The Other God*. London: Yale University Press. 2000.

Taylor, Charles. *Sources of the Self*. Harvard University Press. Cambridge. 1987.

Vlastos, Gregory. *The Philosophy of Socrates*. New York: Anchor Books. 1971.

Watson, *Dark Nature*. New York. HarperPerennial.1997.

Weber, Max. *The Protestant Ethic and the Spirit of Capitalism*. Routledge. New York. 1992.

White, Nicholas. *Plato on Knowledge and Reality*. Hackett. Cambridge. 1976.

Williams, George C. *Adaptation and Natural Selection*. Princeton, NJ. Princeton University Press. 1966.

Woodbridge, Ray. *The Next World War: Tribes, Cities, Nations, and Ecological Decline*. Toronto. University of Toronto Press. 2004.

Young, Dudley. *Origins of the Sacred; The Ecstasies of Love and War*. New York. St. Martin's Press. 1991.

Zaehner, R.C. *The Dawn and Twilight of Zoroastrianism*, London: Phoenix Press. 1961.

INDEX

salvational evil, 5
Sapolsky, Robert M., 54
Sharon, Ariel, 143
Shock and Awe, 46, 144
Socrates, 9, 11-14, 22, 40, 52, 65-70, 72, 76-
   82, 114, 124, 125, 134, 149, 150
Spinoza, Baruch, 3, 4, 11, 103
Stalin, Joseph, 28, 143
strife, 4, 9, 50

T

taboo, 8
Thales, 36
Third Reich, 28, 153
Thrasymachus, 65, 78
Tukhē (Honor), 132

U

Ulysses, 137

V

vita activa, 85
Vlastos, Gregory, 9

W

Watson, Lyall, 51, 52, 63
Weil, Simone, 5
Woodridge, Ray, 63
World Trade Center, 1, 106

X

Xenophon, 130

Y

Yahweh, 135
Young, Dudley, 114, 116, 118